CATHOLIC UNIVERSITY OF AMERICA
CANON LAW STUDIES
NUMBER 42

ORATORIES

A DISSERTATION

Submitted to the Faculty of Canon Law of the Catholic University of America in partial fulfilment of the requirements for the Degree of

DOCTOR OF CANON LAW

by

ALOYSIUS H. FELDHAUS, J. C. L.
Priest of the
Society of the Most Precious Blood

CATHOLIC UNIVERSITY OF AMERICA
WASHINGTON, D. C.
1927

Nihil Obstat:

✠THOMAS J. SHAHAN, S. T. D.,

Censor Deputatus.

Washingtonii, D. C., die 4 Maii, 1927.

Imprimatur:

✠MICHAEL J. CURLEY,

Archiepiscopus Baltimorensis.

Baltimorae, die 4 Maii, 1927.

Cum Permissu Superiorum.

TABLE OF CONTENTS.

BIBLIOGRAPHY.

Juridical Sources.

Acta Apostolicae Sedis, Rome, 1909-1927.

Acta Sanctae Sedis, Rome, 1865-1908.

Breviarium Romanum, Rome, 1924.

Bullarium Benedicti XIV, 13 vols., Mechlin, 1827.

Caeremoniale Episcoporum, Rome, 1886.

Codex Juris Canonici, Rome, 1917.

Codicis Juris Canonici Fontes, 4 vols., Rome, 1923-1926.

Collectanea S. Congregationis de Propaganda Fide, Rome, 1893; 2 vols., Rome, 1907.

Collectio Conclusionum et Resolutionum S. Congregationis Concilii, (Pallottini), 17 vols., Rome, 1868-1893.

Concilii Plenarii Baltimorensis II Acta et Decreta, Baltimore, 1868.

Concilii Plenarii Baltimorensis III Acta et Decreta, Baltimore, 1886.

Corpus Juris Canonici, Editio Lipsiensis II, (Richter-Friedberg) 2 vols., Leipsic, 1922.

Corpus Juris Civilis Justiniani, 3 vols., Berlin, 1912.

Decreta Authentica Congregationis Sacrorum Rituum, 4 vols., (Gardellini, Editio Tertia) Rome, 1856-1879; 6 vols., Rome, 1898-1912.

Missale Romanum, Rome, 1920.

Pontificale Romanum, Mechlin, 1895.

Rituale Romanum, Rome, 1925.

Sacrosancti et Oecumenici Concilii Tridentini Canones et Decreta, (Editio Tertia Chiffletius) Paris, 1910.

Reference Works.

A Coronata, Matthaeus, *De Locis et Temporibus Sacris,* Turin, 1922.

Assemani, Josephus, *De Ecclesiis earum Reverentia et Asylo,* Rome, 1766.

Atchley, Cuthbert, *Ordo Romanus Primus,* London, 1905.

Augustine, Charles, *A Commentary on Canon Law,* 2 ed., 8 vols., St. Louis, 1923.

Barbosa, Augustinus, *De Officio et Potestate Episcopi,* Partes III, 2 vols., Lyons, 1656.

Jus Ecclesiasticum Universum, L. 3, Lyons, 1660.

Barin, Aloisius, *Commentarium ad Canones C. I. C. sacram Liturgiam spectantes,* "Ephemerides Liturgicae," XXXV-XL (1921-1926), Rome.

Benedict XIV, *De Sacrosancto Missae Sacrificio,* L. 3, Prati, 1843.

De Synodo Dioecesana, 2 vols., Rome, 1856.

Beyerlinck, Laurentius, *Magnum Theatrum Vitae Humanae,* 8 vols., Lyons, 1656.

Bingham, Joseph, *Antiquities of the Christian Church,* 10 vols., Oxford, 1855.

Blat, Albertus, *Commentarium Textus Codicis Juris Canonici,* 5 vols., Rome, 1925.

Bona, J., *Rerum Liturgicarum Libri II,* Rome, 1671.

Bouuaert-Simenon, *Manuale Juris Canonici,* Rome, 1924.

Brehm, Franciscus, *Synopsis Additionum et Variationum in Editione Typica Missalis Romani,* Ratisbon, 1920.

Callewaert, C., *Caeremoniale in Missa Privata et Solemni,* Rome, 1922.

Capobianco, Albertus, *Institutionum Juris Canonici Libri III,* Naples, 1766.

Cappello, Felix, *De Sacramentis,* 3 vols., Turin, 1921-1923.

Catholic Encyclopedia, 15 vols., New York, 1907.

Cavalieri, Joannes, *Opera Liturgica,* tom. 5, Venice, 1758.

Cocchi, Guidus, *Commentarium in Codicem Juris Canonici,* 9 vols., Turin, 1924-1927.

De Bonis, Josephus, *De Oratoriis Publicis,* Milan, 1761.

Devoti, Joannes, *Institutionum Canonicarum Libri IV,* Naples, 1860.

Du Cange, Ch., *Glossarium ad Scriptores Mediae et Infimae Latinitatis,* 6 vols., Paris, 1738.

Duchesne, L., *Origines du Culte Chrétien,* Paris, 1902.

Fagnani, Prosperus, *Commentaria in Libros Decretalium,* 4 vols., Venice, 1697.

Fanfani, Ludovicus, *De Jure Religiosorum,* Turin, 1925.

Farinacius, Prosperus, *De Immunitate Ecclesiarum,* Rome, 1621.

Fattolilli, J., *Theatrum Immunitatis et Libertatis Ecclesiasticae,* Rome, 1714.

Ferraris, Lucius, *Prompta Bibliotheca Juridica, Canonica, Moralis,* 9 vols., Rome, 1885.

Ferreres, Joannes, *Compendium Theologiae Moralis,* 2 vols., Barcelona, 1923.
Institutiones Canonicae, 2 vols., Barcelona, 1920.

Fortunatus a Brixia, *De Oratoriis Domesticis,* Rome, 1766.

Gasparri, Petrus, *De Sanctissima Eucharistia,* 2 vols., Paris, 1897.

Gasquet, Francis, *Parish Life in Mediaeval England,* New York, 1906.

Gattico, Joannes, *De Oratoriis Domesticis,* Rome, 1746.

Graesse, J., *Orbis Latinus,* Berlin, 1909.

Ligouri, St. Alphonse, *Theologia Moralis,* L. 7, Rome, 1891.

Mansi, Joannes, *Sacrorum Conciliorum Nova et Amplissima Collectio,* 51 vols., Paris, 1902-1924.

Many, S., *Praelectiones de Locis Sacris,* Paris, 1904.
Praelectiones de Missa, Paris, 1903.

MARTENE, Edmundus, *De Antiquis Ecclesiae Ritibus*, 4 vols., Rouen, 1700.

MARTIGNY, A., *Dictionnaire des Antiquités Chrétiennes*, Paris, 1877.

MARTINUCCI-MENGHINI, *Manuale Sacrarum Caeremoniarum*, L. 8, Rome, 1916.

MIGNE, J., *Patrologia Graeca*, 161 vols., Paris, 1866.
Patrologia Latina, 231 vols., Paris, 1864.

MOCCHEGIANI, Petrus, *Jurisprudentia Ecclesiastica*, 3 vols., Freiburg, 1905.

MOSTAZO, Franciscus de, *De Causis Piis*, L. 8, Lyons, 1686.

PASQUALIGO, Zacharias, *De Sacrificio*, 2 vols., Venice, 1707.

PETRA, Vincentius, *Commentaria ad Constitutiones Apostolicas*, 5 vols., Venice, 1729.

PIGNATELLI, Jacobus, *Consultationes Canonicae*, 11 vols., Coloniae Allogobrorum, 1700.

PIRHING, Henricus, *Jus Canonicum Nova Methodo Explicatum*, 4 vols., Dillingen, 1722.

POMEROY, John, *Equity Jurisprudence*, 2 vols., San Francisco, 1905.

PRUEMMER, Dominicus, *Manuale Juris Canonici*, Freiburg, 1922.
Manuale Theologiae Moralis, 3 vols., Freiburg, 1923.

RAUS, P. J., *Institutiones Canonicae*, Paris, 1923.

REIFFENSTUEL, Anacletus, *Jus Canonicum Universum*, 4 vols., Venice, 1735.

SCHMALZGRUEBER, Franciscus, *Jus Ecclesiasticum Universum*, 12 vols., Rome, 1844.

SMITH-CHEETHAM, *Dictionary of Christian Antiquities*, 2 vols., Hartford, 1880.

SUAREZ, Franciscus, *Opera Omnia*, 26 vols., Paris, 1866.

THALHOFER, Valentinus, *Handbuch der Katholischen Liturgik*, 2 vols., Freiburg, 1883.

THOMASSINUS, L., *Vetus et Nova Disciplina circa Beneficia et Beneficiarios,* L. 9 in 3 vols., Paris, 1688.

TUSCHUS, D., *Practicae Conclusiones Juris,* 7 vols., Lyons, 1634.

VAN DE BURGT, P., *De Celebratione Missarum,* Ultrajecti, 1871.

VAN DER STAPPEN, J., *Sacra Liturgia,* 5 vols., Mechlin, 1903.

VAN ESPEN, Zegerus B., *Jus Ecclesiasticum Universum,* L. 10, Venice, 1769.

Scripta Omnia, 4 vols., Louvain, 1753.

VAN GAMEREN, Adolphus, *De Oratoriis Publicis et Privatis,* Louvain, 1861.

VERANI, Cajetanus, *Juris Canonici Universi Commentarius Paratitlarius,* 3 vols., Monachii, 1703.

VERMEERSCH-CREUSEN, *Epitome Juris Canonici,* 2 ed., 3 vols., Rome, 1925.

WALCOTT, M., *Sacred Archaeology,* London, 1868.

WAPELHORST, Innocentius, *Compendium Sacrae Liturgiae,* 9 ed., New York, 1915.

WERNZ, Franciscus, *Jus Decretalium,* 2 ed., tom. 6 in 9 vols., Rome, 1914.

WILKINS, David, *Consilia Magnae Britanniae et Hiberniae,* 4 vols., London, 1737.

WILSON, George, *International Law,* New York, 1922.

WOYWOD, Stanislaus, *A Practical Commentary on the Code of Canon Law,* 2 vols., New York, 1925.

The New Canon Law, New York, 1918.

WUEST-MULLANEY, *Matters Liturgical,* New York, 1926.

ZITELLI, Zephyrn, *Apparatus Juris Canonici,* L. 2, Rome, 1888.

PERIODICALS.

COMMENTARIUM PRO RELIGIOSIS, Rome, 1920-1927.

EPHEMERIDES LITURGICAE, Rome, 1887-1927.

HOMILETIC AND PASTORAL REVIEW, New York, 1904-1927.

PART I.

Pre-Code Names, Definitions, Origin and Kinds of Oratories.

Introduction.

History clearly shows that the cult of worship which man as a dependent creature owes to his divine Creator usually has been offered in some special place set aside for and sacred to the fulfilment of this holy duty. In the Book of Genesis there are indications of this fact, one of the most pronounced examples being that which gives the origin of the famous place of worship at Bethel.[1] The various places selected as sacred by the Chosen People either on their own initiative or at the express command of God can be traced in Holy Writ, until finally the wonderful Tabernacle of the Desert was succeeded by Solomon's magnificent Temple at Jerusalem.[2]

This custom of the Chosen People of having special places of worship is found likewise in almost every other race known to history. Just as each nation retained some idea of a divine being to whom it offered allegiance and worship, so also each possessed some place or places which in a special way were considered sacred to that deity and were, as a consequence, excluded from profane use.[3] Here it erected a shrine or temple in which the various rites and ceremonies were observed according to the cult and ritual of the god in question. History has recorded, and modern archaeological research still is discovering many such places of worship, some of which are splendid monuments of ancient architecture, and all of which plainly indicate that man, whether he did or did

1 Cf. Gen., XXVIII, 16-22 and XXXI, 13.
2 Cf. Ex., XXVI; III Kings, VI.
3 Cf. Assemani, *De Ecclesiis*, § 1, n. 1.

not realize that he owed God worship at all places and times, nevertheless chose certain special places as best suited for rendering such worship.

With the coming of Christ the nature of these places was indeed changed, but the underlying idea of certain places being set aside for divine worship was retained. For the very nature of divine cult as something essentially sacred seems to presuppose not only that it be holily performed, but also that it be performed in a place that is sacred and free from profane use. Hence it is but natural that practically all of the early Christian writers testify to the existence of such special places of worship.

It is true that apparently contrary statements can be found in the works of Arnobius,[4] Origen[5] and Minucius Felix,[6] which assert that the Christians had neither temples nor altars and that God should be worshipped in all places, His best altar and temple being the heart of man. The three works in which these passages are found are essentially polemic, direct attacks on pagan excesses rather than apologies for and explanations of Christianity. What evidently is meant in these statements is that the Christians had no temples in the pagan sense of the word; this was indeed true, for the Christian places of worship were radically different from the pagan temples which, as these same authors strongly emphasize, were disgraced by scenes of utter licentiousness. The Christian's heart is truly God's best temple, but the love and reverence, he, as an individual, inwardly feels toward God, he outwardly expresses as a member of society in the Christian place of worship. God should be worshipped in every place, but this does not militate against the fact that Christianity always has considered certain places as particularly adapted to the rendering of such worship. Hence, these few passages cannot be interpreted literally and strictly, as there is extant positive and in-

---

[4] *Disputat. adv. Gentes,* L. 6, c. 1; M. P. L., V, 1162.
[5] *Contra Celsum,* L. 8, c. 17-19; M. P. G., XI, 1540-1546.
[6] *Octav.,* c. 10, 32; M. P. L., III, 264, 339.

controvertible evidence for the existence of special places of worship at the time of and prior to these writers; moreover, they, themselves, give similar testimony elsewhere in their works.[7]

---

[7] Cf. Arnobius, *Disputat. adv. Gentes,* L. 4, c. 36; M. P. L., V, 1076; Origen, *Hom. X, in Jos.;* M. P. G., XII, 880.

CHAPTER I.

Names for Places of Worship.

In the first centuries of the Christian era, the sacred places in which the Christians worshipped were known by various names which were used synonymously as is expressly stated in the Roman Breviary: "Jam ab Apostolorum tempore loca fuerunt Deo dicata, quae a quibusdam Oratoria, ab aliis Ecclesiae dicebantur, ubi collectae fiebant per unam sabbati, et christianus populus orare, Dei verbum audire, et Eucharistiam sumere solitus erat."[1] The names most frequently used by the early Christians thus interchangeably were:

1) **Basilica**: St. Isidore of Seville not only applies this term to Christian places of worship, but also offers a reason from etymology for the use thereof: "Ideo divina templa basilicae nominantur, quia ibi Regi (βασιλεῖ) omnium Deo cultus et sacrificia offeruntur."[2] Before the time of St. Isidore this term was used in the writings of St. Ambrose,[3] St. Augustine[4] and other Fathers. Bingham,[5] offering a historical reason for the use of this term, states that the word basilica was used by the Romans to designate public buildings, especially the courts of judicature, but that many of them were given to the Church after the conversion of Constantine and changed into places of Christian worship, retaining their original name. Less valuable is Bona's[6] suggestion that this name was given to Christian places of worship because of the magnificence of the edifice, as it was applied indiscriminately to all Christian places of worship, many of which at the early date when this term was used, were far from being magnificent. Later this term was applied

---

1 Lect. IV, *In Dedicatione SS. Salvatoris;* Nov. 9.
2 *Etymol.*, L. 15, c. 4; M. P. L., LXXXII, 545.
3 *De Basilicis Tradendis;* M. P. L., XVI, 1007.
4 *Sermo de Diversis,* n. 356; M. P. L., XXXIX, 1578.
5 *Antiquities of the Christian Church,* L. 8, c. 1.
6 *Rer. Liturg.*, L. 1, c. 19, n. 4.

exclusively to churches that were endowed with special privileges by the Roman Pontiff.

2) **Dominicum** (domus Domini, κυριακή, κυριακόν[7]): This term was employed already by St. Cyprian[8] who, however, applied it not only to a place of worship, but also to the Lord's Supper and to the Lord's Day. Though it was used also by other Fathers,[9] it never was in general use.

3) **Templum** (ναός): This name was not used by the Christians of the first three centuries to denote their places of worship lest confusion arise in distinguishing the pagan places of worship from their own.[10] But with the advent of peace to the Church under Constantine and the ensuing decline of paganism, there was no longer any hesitation in applying it to Christian places of worship as is evident from the writings of many of the Fathers of the fourth and fifth centuries.[11] In Holy Scripture it was used frequently without any modification to denote the Temple of Jerusalem,[12] while Christ Himself used it in reference to His own body.[13]

Fanum, a term in very general use among the pagans to denote the temples of the gods, never was adopted by the Christians who reserved it as a name for the heathen temples and occasionally used it by way of contempt in referring to the places of worship of heretics.[14]

4) **Ecclesia** (ἐκκλησία): This was the term most frequently used by the early Christians. In its original meaning as used by the Greeks from whom it was derived,

---

7 From these Greek terms are derived with but slight variation the Saxon *Kyrik* or *Kyrch,* the Scotch *Kirk,* the Flemish *Kerck,* the German *Kirche* and the English *Church;* cf. Many, *De Locis Sacris,* n. 2.

8 *De Opere et Eleemosynis,* n. 15; M. P. L., IV, 613.

9 Cf. St. Jerome, *Chronicon;* M. P. L., XXVII, 677; Eusebius of Caesarea, *Hist. Eccl.,* L. 9, c. 2; M. P. G., XX, 833.

10 Thalhofer, *Handbuch der Katholischen Liturgik,* I, c. 6, § 55.

11 Cf. St. Ambrose, *Ad Marcel.,* ep. 20; M. P. L., XVI, 995; St. Augustine, *De Civitate Dei,* L. 8, c. 27; M. P. L., XLI, 255; Lactantius, *Instit.,* L. 5, c. 2; M. P. L., VI, 553.

12 Cf. Matt., XXIII, 16, 17, 35; XXVII, 40; John, II, 19, 20.

13 Cf. John, II, 21.

14 Cf. St. Ambrose, *Ad Theodosium,* ep. 40; M. P. L., XVI, 1107.

it referred rather to the assembly of people met together upon sacred or civil affairs than to the place or building in which the meeting was held. Thus, Isidore of Pelusium accurately distinguishes "the *ecclesiasterion* [which] is the temple or building made of wood and stone" from "the *ecclesia* [which] is the congregation of persons that meet in the *ecclesiasterion.*"[15] Though this original meaning of "ecclesia" occasionally was retained both in Holy Scripture[16] and by the Fathers,[17] even as it is also today, it was used in its figurative or transferred meaning of "ecclesiasterion" by practically every writer of Christian antiquity who had occasion to refer to a Christian place of worship. Just as the term temple in the first three centuries when used without any further qualification referred to a pagan place of worship and the term synagogue to a Jewish one, so also did the term "ecclesia" refer to a Christian place of worship. The three words in themselves were understood to connote the kind of religion to which the respective places of worship were devoted.

5) **Oratorium** (oratoriolum, oraculum, domus orationis, *εὐκτήριον, οἶκος εὐκτήριος, προσευκτηρία*): Referring to the Temple of Jerusalem and quoting Isaias,[18] our divine Saviour said: "Domus mea domus orationis vocabitur."[19] It is from these words of Christ that the Christians derived the above group of names which they very frequently used in reference to their places of worship. Of the many early writers who used these terms, the following may be cited: Socrates: "Constantine ordered an oratory (*οἶκον εὐκτήριον*) to be built under Abraham's oak and another church (*ἑτέραν ἐκκλησίαν*) at Heliopolis;"[20] Eusebius: "When peace was restored to the Church there were feasts of dedication

15 *Ad Theodosium*, L. 2, ep. 246; M. P. G., LXXVIII, 685.
16 Cf. Philemon, I, 2.
17 Cf. St. Cyril, *Catech.*, XVIII, n. 24; M. P. G., XXXIII, 1044.
18 LVI, 7.
19 Matt., XXI, 13; Luke, XIX, 46.
20 *Hist. Eccl.*, L. 1, c. 18; M. P. G., LXVII, 124.

in every city and consecrations of newly built oratories (προσευκτηρίων);"[21] Gregory the Great: "Cassius of Narni shortly before his death offered Mass in the oratory of his episcopal residence (in episcopii oratorio fecit Missam)."[22] Not only is the term "oratorium" used, but also its appropriateness when applied to places of worship is commented upon by St. Augustine: "In oratorio nemo aliquid agat nisi id ad quod est factum, unde et nomen accepit;"[23] and also in the Rule of St. Benedict:[24] "Oratorium hoc sit quod dicitur, nec quidquam ibi aliud geratur aut condatur."[25] At times, however, though rarely, it was used with an entirely different meaning. Thus in the earliest extant "Ordo Romanus" supposed to have been compiled about the year 730, it is used with the meaning of a *prie dieu* as is evident from § 8: "Quartus scholae praecedit Pontificem ut ponat oratorium ante altare, et accedens Pontifex orat super ipsum."[26]

6) **Cappella:** This term, as Gattico[27] observes, is used by no writer prior to the Seventh Century. The more common explanation for its origin is based on an incident in the life of St. Martin of Tours. Sulpicius Severus[28] tells us that St. Martin while on his way to church was met by a beggar who asked for alms in the form of clothes. The holy bishop told the deacon who accompanied him to tend to the man's needs and proceeded into the church. Later the beggar came and complained that the deacon had failed to help him whereupon St. Martin gave him part of his own outer garment;[29] this piece of clothing was part of the mon-

---

21 *Hist. Eccl.*, L. 10, c. 3; M. P. G., XX, 848.

22 *Hom. 37 de Evang.;* M. P. L., LXXVI, 1281.

23 Ep. 211; M. P. L., XXXIII, 960.

24 C. 52; M. P. L., LXVI, 747.

25 To which Gratian, c. 6, D. XLII, added: "*Quam quod divinis ministeriis conveniat.*"

26 Atchley, *Ordo Romanus Primus,* Appendix I, 128.

27 *De Oratoriis Domesticis*, c. 2, n. 1.

28 *Dialog*, II, c. 1; M. P. L., XX, 201.

29 Compare this narrative with the slightly different but better known version contained in the Breviary, Lect. IV, *In Fest. S. Martini;* Nov. 11.

astic habit and was called a "cuculla" or "cappa." After the Saint's death this "cappa" having been recovered was religiously preserved by the French kings; the sacred ministers entrusted with the care of this and other relics of the Saint were known as "cappellani," and the place where these relics were preserved was called a "cappella." Later any place or room that contained relics, sacred things, precious vessels, etc., was called a "cappella," and from this the transition to "cappella" in the meaning of an oratory or place of worship was easy and natural.[30] Various other explanations have been offered for the origin of this term; thus De Bonis[31] derives it from "capsa" or "capa," a reliquary or casket in which relics are preserved; Beyerlinck[32] derives it from the fact that smaller places of worship often were roofed with the skins of goats ("capellae") even as the Jewish Temple was roofed with the skins of goats and rams;[33] Barbosa[34] offers the same explanation, suggesting its derivation from "capra," while Walcott[35] reverts to the reliquary theory of De Bonis, substituting "cupella" for "capsa." But whatever its origin may have been, this term has been in general use since the Seventh Century.

After the terms church and oratory had acquired separate and distinct meanings, the term chapel usually was employed synonymously with oratory, though at different times a distinction was made in the use of the two terms. Thus Gattico[36] affirms that in England during the Middle Ages the term "oratorium" was used only for what we now call private oratories, while "cappella" was reserved for what are now known as public oratories. Many authors used the term "cappella" to designate shrines situated within or structurally forming part of large

30 Cf. Capobianco, *Institutiones*, L. 2, Tit. 8, § 3.
31 *De Oratoriis Publicis*, n. 13.
32 *Magnum Theatrum*, II, s. v. "Cappella."
33 Cf. Ex., XXXV, 6-7 and XXXVI, 14-19.
34 *Jus Eccl. Univers.*, L. 2, c. 8, n. 19.
35 *Sacred Archaeology*, p. 136.
36 *De Oratoriis Dom.*, c. 2, n. 6.

churches and applied the term "oratorium" to separate and detached places of worship. This latter distinction is still observed to some extent, though usually the two terms are used interchangeably by those versed in ecclesiastical terminology, while the ordinary faithful generally use the term chapel in referring to any place of worship which is not a church.

The above are the most important names for the early Christian places of worship, though there were also others used among which it may be of interest to mention: *Concilium,*[37] which soon was used exclusively in the meaning of a legitimate ecclesiastical council or synod; *Conventiculum,*[38] and *Conciliabulum,*[39] which later were restricted to heretical or schismatic assemblies. The terms *Martyrium, Confessio* and *Memoria*[40] were reserved for churches or oratories erected over the grave of a martyr, or for those that possessed his relics or at least were named in his honor; but if the person in memory of whom the sacred place was erected was one of the Apostles or Prophets, it was called an *Apostoleum*[41] or a *Propheteum;*[42] and Sozomen[43] uses *Michaelium* to designate an oratory erected in honor of the Archangel Michael. The term *Titulus,* so frequently found in such official books as the Breviary and the Pontifical, as a rule was applied only to churches situated in Rome. Various explanations[44] have been suggested for the origin and precise meaning of this term, but not one of them is conclusive or explains why the term was used more generally at Rome than elsewhere.

---

37 Cf. Gaudentius, *Sermo 17;* M. P. L., XX, 971.
38 Cf. Arnobius, *Disputat. adv. Gentes,* L. 4, c. 36; M. P. L., V, 1076.
39 Cf. St. Jerome, *In Zachar.,* c. 8; M. P. L., XXV, 1467.
40 Cf. St. Augustine, *De Civitate Dei,* L. 8, c. 27; M. P. L., XXII, 255.
41 Cf. Sozomen, *Hist. Eccl.,* L. 9, c. 10; M. P. G., LXVII, 1617.
42 Cf. Theodorus Lector, *Hist. Eccl.,* L. 2, n. 63; M. P. G., LXXXVI, 213.
43 *Hist. Eccl.,* L. 2, c. 3; M. P. G., LXVII, 940.
44 Cf. Thomassinus, *Vet. et Nov. Disc.,* Pars. I, L. 2, c. 21, n. 11; Cavalieri, *Opera Liturgica,* L. 1, c. 2, n. 33.

CHAPTER II.

The Origin of Oratories.

As was stated in the previous chapter, the various names given there were used synonymously in the early Church to designate any place of Christian worship. It would be absurd to expect to find in the early Church the precise distinctions that were made during the subsequent centuries in the different types of places of worship and in the names that were assigned exclusively to each. Such variety in places of divine worship with its corresponding finesse in ecclesiastical terminology could arise only after centuries of peace and prosperity with their accompanying development of a more and more varied and rich external cult.

At first the Apostles used the Temple of Jerusalem in which to preach the Gospel of Christ; though they were arrested and called to account for this, they continued to do so.[1] But there is no indication in Holy Writ that they performed the Eucharistic rite in the Temple. On the contrary, St. Luke [2] seems to insinuate that they did not, for to his statement that the believers held all their goods in common and continued with one accord in the Temple, he immediately adds that they broke bread from house to house, which apparently implies that the Eucharistic cult was offered in the private homes of the faithful of the New rather than in the Temple of the Old Dispensation. When the Apostles extended their missionary labors beyond Jerusalem, they frequently used the local synagogues in which to address the people, but after a number were converted, the faithful met in private homes for the performance of their religious rites as is clearly indicated in the Epistles of St. Paul.[3]

1 Cf. Acts, III, 1-12, IV, 1-7 and V, 21, 42.
2 Acts, II, 44-46.
3 Cf. Rom., XVI, 3-5; I Cor., XVI, 19; Col., IV, 15; Philemon, I, 2.

This practice of using private dwellings as places of divine worship [4] continued more or less unchanged throughout the Apostolic and the sub-Apostolic Age. But during the persecutions which were instituted against the Christians, even the ordinary private dwellings seldom were sufficiently safe for the performance of their religious duties. Then it was that they chose the most deserted and least suspected places for holding their services;[5] these they would abandon as soon as there was any likelihood of discovery. During a lull in the persecutions the Christians for the first time were given permission to erect sacred edifices in the public places of Rome by Alexander Severus (222-223). This grant, however, was soon recalled by subsequent emperors, notably by Valerian. But from the time of Valerian's death (260) until the persecution of Diocletian (303)—except for a short interval in the reign of Aurelian (270-275)—the Christians were left undisturbed, and during this comparatively long period of peace "they erected ample oratories and spacious churches in every city," as Eusebius of Caesarea [6] testifies. These, however, were again destroyed or at least closed during the terrible persecution under Diocletian. The conversion of Constantine and the Edict of Milan (313), in virtue of which Christianity was given state recognition, at length brought lasting peace. Countless and magnificent public churches [7] were erected throughout the empire, but many of the sacred places in private homes still were retained and used for divine worship,[8] and in this fact probably can be found the beginning of what was soon to constitute the important division of places of divine worship into churches and oratories.

---

[4] Duchesne (*Origines du Culte Chrétien,* c. 12, § 1) gives a very good description of these primitive churches in private houses.

[5] Cf. Martene, *De Antiquis Ecclesiae Ritibus,* L. 1, c. 3, art. 5, n. 3.

[6] *Hist. Eccl.,* L. 8, c. 1; M. P. G., XX, 741.

[7] Cf. Eusebius, *De Vita Constantini,* L. 4, c. 58 (M. P. G., XX, 1209), for a description of the world renowned "Ecclesia Constantiniana."

[8] Cf. Martigny, *Dictionnaire des Antiquités Chrétiennes,* s. v. "Oratoires Domestiques."

For up to this time, as has been emphasized, the terms church and oratory did not represent a real distinction, as the same sacred place was referred to by both names, even as it was called also "Dominicum," "Basilica," "Concilium," etc. But after the conversion of Constantine with the peace and prosperity which that happy event brought to the Church, these terms began to assume specific meanings. The term church became restricted to public edifices of worship; these were erected or at least used exclusively for divine service, and gradually were further distinguished as cathedral or parochial churches according as they were presided over by a bishop or by a priest. The term oratory, however, came to be applied to those places of worship that were of a more or less private character, especially to those that were retained or erected in private homes. Unfortunately, it is necessary to add that even after these terms had acquired specifically different meanings, they nevertheless—though less frequently—were used interchangeably, thereby giving rise to much doubt and confusion; thus as late as the Seventeenth Century Mostazo still could assert: "Vox oratorium in Ecclesia Dei aliquando generaliter pro qualibet sacra aede usurpatur." [9]

A further distinction between these two types of sacred edifices arose from the conversion of the nobility and from the institution of the Religious Orders. Both classes erected places of worship on their estates which were intended to serve their own religious needs rather than those of the faithful at large; hence arose a further distinction between churches and oratories based upon the purpose for which they were erected—whether for the benefit of all the faithful or whether they were intended primarily for a certain class. There was another means of differentiation which, though based on something purely accidental, was in the popular estimation and in common parlance of prime importance: the larger and more magnificent places of worship were called churches, the smaller and less imposing ones were called oratories.

---

[9] *De Causis Piis*, L. 5, c. 10, n. 1.

This method of differentiation, though devoid of juridical foundation, as a matter of fact often proved correct, for frequently the churches in the juridical meaning of the term were the larger and more imposing edifices.

The development of these elements of difference between churches and oratories was naturally very gradual and today its progress can be but vaguely traced because of our very limited sources of information on the subject. However, the actual fact that a distinction was made between them soon after the persecutions ceased is certain; for the ecclesiastical and even the civil authorities began placing certain limitations on oratories which were not applied to churches, and this fact clearly indicates that both authorities recognized a distinction between the two classes of sacred places. These restrictions consisted especially in limiting the number and kind of liturgical functions that could be celebrated in oratories. At times and places these limitations were so universal as to reduce the oratories in reality to that which their name etymologically signifies—places of prayer. Various causes contributed to the passing of such legislative restrictions of which mention need be made here only of the relatively small number of priests who were, therefore, needed in the public churches, the danger of abuses in the performance of the sacred functions in more or less private places of worship and finally that these restrictions served as a means of combating such heretical and schismatic sects as the Eustachians and the Anomaeans who held their assemblies and performed their religious rites in private houses.[10] But even when this legislation was most restrictive, the oratories did not cease to exist and gradually other means were adopted to correct the above and kindred abuses.

10 Cf. Gattico, *De Oratoriis Dom.*, c. 4, n. 7; Van Espen, *Scholia in Synodum Gangrensem*, *Opera Omnia*, IV, Pars 2.

CHAPTER III.

Church and Oratory; Definitions and Differences.

In view of the origin and gradual development of the distinction between churches and oratories, it is not surprising that early authors either avoided defining them or that the definitions and descriptions which they offered are rather vague and unsatisfactory. Many authors divided churches and oratories into their respective species and gave fairly good definitions of each without defining churches and oratories themselves. The few definitions that were attempted were either too comprehensive or too restrictive.

As an example of the former, the assertion of Barin can be cited here: "Ecclesia ab antiquis definitur: Locus sacer murorum ambitu circumdatus."[1] It is patent that this definition is so comprehensive as to include not only churches but also oratories and even cemeteries which at a very early age were considered as sacred places and usually were surrounded by walls. As an example of the too restrictive definition the traditional one of an oratory can be alleged as quoted by De Bonis: "Oratorii nomine Sacrorum Canonum periti designant locum idoneum ad orandum, precesque Deo offerendas, quem in propria domo eligere cuilibet permittitur."[2] This definition evidently can refer only to oratories used for prayer alone, as the same authors who offer it invariably add in the course of their treatise: "Missas autem ibi celebrare non licet."[3] For the celebration of the holy Sacrifice in such oratories erected on private authority was strictly forbidden already in very early times.[4]

---

1 *Commentarium, Eph. Liturg.*, XXXVI (1922), 145.
2 *De Oratoriis Pub.*, n. 1.
3 C. 33, D. 1, *de cons.*
4 Cf. the particular legislation given in Chapter V, Article 3.

The above definitions were retained for many centuries, but gradually new ones were introduced and authors began to contrast the concepts of church and oratory in order to discover in what and in how far they differed from each other. Thus Barbosa defines a church as "aedes publica auctoritate constituta, in quam Christiani ad rem divinam audiendam et sacramenta suscipienda conveniant."[5] Similar to this definition are those of Verani: "Ecclesia est aedes publica deputata auctoritate Episcopi divino cultui exercendo et praesertim Missae Sacrificio celebrando;"[6] of Du Cange: "Ecclesia est aedes sacra publico pietatis exercitio et cultui divino destinata, in quam convenit fidelium coetus;"[7] and of Ferraris: "Ecclesia est aedes publica cultui divino deputata, in qua fideles ad colendum et invocandum Deum, divina administranda et percipienda conveniunt."[8] That these definitions were a great improvement on the older one cited above from Barin is very evident.

Unfortunately, however, the same progress cannot be discovered in the definitions that were offered of an oratory. Most authors contented themselves with treating and defining the kinds of oratories and either did not essay a definition of the genus oratory, or they quoted the traditional definition of a "Locus aptus ad orandum."[9] Among the few definitions that amplified the traditional one or marked a complete departure from it, attention need be called only to those of Tuschus: "Oratorium dicitur privatus locus in quo orari potest et de licentia Episcopi potest celebrari;"[10] and of Du Cange: "Oratoria dicta sunt privatae aedes sacrae in agris et villis exstructae, quae parochiarum jus non habebant . . . Oratoria dicebantur in quibus nec baptismus celebrari, nec sacramenta fidelibus ministrari fas erat, sed tantum Missae a cappellanis fiebant."[11]

---

5 *Jus Eccl. Univers.*, L. 2, c. 1, n. 14.

6 *Commentarius Paratitlarius*, III, Tit. 48, § 1, n. 2.

7 *Glossarium*, III, s. v. "Ecclesia."

8 *Bibliotheca*, III, s. v. "Ecclesia," art. 1, n. 1.

9 Cf. Ferraris, *Bibliotheca*, V, s. v. "Oratorium," n. 1.

10 *Practicae Conclusiones Juris*, V, s. 1. O, Concl. 175.

11 *Glossarium*, IV, s. v. "Oratorium"; II, s. v. "Cardinalis."

While not offering a definition of an oratory, Pirhing thus differentiates it from a church: "Porro haec est inter oratorium et ecclesiam differentia, quod ecclesia dicitur, quae principaliter deputatur ad celebrationem Missae, et ad orandum, et consecratur per Episcopum, cui etiam constituta est certa dos, pro clericis in illa deservientibus, et pro aliis necessitatibus; Oratorium vero non consecratur, nec constituitur ei dos, nec erigitur principaliter, ut ibi celebretur, sed tantum ut oretur, ideoque sine licentia Episcopi non potest in istis oratoriis Missa celebrari."[12] Tuschus, after giving the definition quoted above, adds in his next Conclusion: "Differt oratorium ab ecclesia: quia ecclesia dicitur, quando certa dos illi est assignata pro sacerdote et clericis qui ibi serviunt, et pro aliis ecclesiae necessitatibus; oratorium, quando habet dotem, et si est constructum sine Episcopo, non potest in eo Missa celebrari; si vero cum licentia est constructum, potest in eo Missa celebrari, non solemniter, neque diebus festivis. . . . Cavere debent habentes oratoria ne illa reducantur ad faciem ecclesiae, et quod non assignent dotem, neque in ea instituant certum rectorem, quia censeretur ecclesia."[13] Quite similar in part are the words of Verani: "Quod si quaeratur, quale sit discrimen inter oratorium et ecclesiam. Respondetur, ecclesiam differre ab oratorio, quia illa principaliter deputatur ad celebrandas Missas et orandum, consecraturque per Episcopum, cui etiam certa constituta est dos pro clericis in illa deservientibus, et pro aliis ecclesiae necessitatibus. Secus oratorium non consecratur, nec ei constituitur dos, neque erigitur principaliter ut ibi celebretur, sed tantum ut oretur, adeo ut sine licentia Episcopi non possit in istis Missa celebrari."[14] And even Fagnani offered a somewhat similar differentiation: "Qaero quae sit differentia inter oratorium et ecclesiam. Ecclesia dicitur ubi statuta est certa dos pro sacerdote et clericis ibi deservientibus, et pro aliis necessitatibus

---

12 *Jus Canonicum*, III, L. 3, Tit. 39, § 3, n. 81.
13 *Practicae Conclusiones Juris*, V, s. 1. O, Concl. 176.
14 *Commentarius Paratitlarius*, III, Tit. 39, § 4, n. 14.

ecclesiae. Oratorium vero dicitur quod non est dotatum, nec est aedificatum ad Missam celebrandam, sed tantummodo ad orandum. . . . Potest in eis quandoque celebrari de licentia Episcopi, qui tamen non debet eam concedere in magnis festivitatibus."[15]

The above definitions and distinctions are good examples of the many laudable attempts that were made to clarify that which in the abstract was a very obscure question. In concrete cases the distinction between the various kinds of sacred edifices usually was made quite easily, certain sacred places being universally recognized as churches, while others just as generally were considered as oratories; thus all admitted that parish and cathedral churches were churches in the strict sense of the word and that the sacred places reserved exclusively for the worship of Religious were oratories. However, at times really doubtful cases arose for which there was no certain and definite method of obtaining a solution except by referring them to the competent ecclesiastical authority. For the definitions and differentiations made by canonists, while true in many cases, were not universal in their application. This was due to the fact that in formulating them they seem to have had the private oratory in mind almost to the exclusion of the public oratory. Thus in the quotations cited above, Pirhing, Verani and Fagnani state that an oratory could be distinguished from a church by the fact that no endowment was assigned to or prescribed for an oratory, and the first two authors declare that an oratory was not to be consecrated. Nevertheless, it is known as certain that some oratories were consecrated and that an endowment was prescribed for such consecrated oratories.[16] However, in justification of the above authors it must be admitted that especially such consecrated and endowed oratories very frequently were considered and called churches.

---

[15] *Commentaria in Libros Decretalium*, c. 27, X, *de censibus*, III, 39.

[16] Cf. Petra, *Commentaria ad Constitutiones Apostolicas*, I, *In Const. 2 Paschalis II*, § 1, n. 95.

Other limitations and defects in the definitions and differentiations that were offered could be suggested, but the above will suffice to indicate that although the distinction of churches and oratories was made in theory and in practice, the theory by no means was perfect and its application consequently led to practical doubts and difficulties.

CHAPTER IV.

KINDS OF ORATORIES.

Until the Nineteenth Century Canon Law and its commentators recognized but two classes of oratories, public and private. Though this distinction had been made for centuries, the precise nature and extent of the two types of oratories was disputed by canonists, though in broad outlines they agreed. In 1899, however, the Congregation of Rites [1] removed all doubts in the matter by not only authoritatively defining public and private oratories, but also by officially recognizing and defining semi-public oratories. Many of the doubts and controversies had been due to the oratories which the decree of 1899 called semi-public; prior to this decree such oratories generally were treated as public, though at times and under certain conditions they were considered as private as Van Gameren implied when he wrote: "Multiplicem autem hae voces [oratoria publica et privata] habent intellectum; unde unam eamdemque aediculam aliquando privatam, aliquando publicam, diverso sub respectu nuncupari contingit." [2]

Though the authors, prior to the decree of 1899, differed greatly in the application of their definitions, they did agree, at least essentially, in the definitions themselves, though also here a few not unimportant differences can be found. To show these facts and to obtain at least a general idea of public and private oratories before investigating the legislation that was enacted concerning them, it will suffice to cite the definitions of the following authors:

Barbosa: "Oratorium publicum dicitur quod in aliquo loco publico ad instar basilicae vel cappellae auctoritate

1 Jan. 23; D. A., 4007.

2 *De Oratoriis*, Pars I, c. 4.

Episcopi est fundatum et habet campanam, et ostium patens in via publica. Oratoria autem privata dicuntur illa quae sunt in domibus privatis, in angulis earum, in quibus oratur, et non habent campanam, neque ostium patens in via publica, . . . quamvis de licentia Missae in illis celebrentur."[3] *Gattico*: "Erit igitur publicum oratorium, quod publico, sive omnium usui patebit; et e contra, privatum, quod aliquorum tantummodo usui parabitur."[4] *Ferraris*: "Oratorium publicum est illud quod auctoritate Episcopi est erectum, et ad Dei cultum tantummodo perpetuo dedicatum, habens aditum et liberum ingressum per viam publicam et pariter egressum in viam communem. Oratorium privatum pro Missis celebrandis est illud quod [est erectum] intra domesticos parietes, in angulis domus privatae, non habens ingressum vel egressum in viam publicam."[5] *Van Gameren*: "Publicum dicitur oratorium quod omnium indiscriminatim usui est accomodatum; privatum vero, quod non ita promiscuum praebet aditum, sed tantum cuidam collegio aut familiae etiam privatae inservit. Ast ut oratorium revera sit atque vocetur ex hoc capite publicum, jura requirunt ut liber omnino ad illud detur ingressus; quae quidem conditio adesse, ad legum canonicarum normam, tunc dicitur, quando aedificii janua immediate publicae et communi adjacet viae."[6]

From the above and similar definitions it is evident that canonists considered that oratory public which had a public entrance, was dedicated to divine worship and was open to all the faithful. On these three requisites they were almost unanimous, though some considered several other things necessary. Barbosa[7] emphasized the necessity of a campanile and bell and in this a few other canonists followed him; but most authors rejected this view, for as Pignatelli correctly observes: "Campana est tan-

---

3 *Jus Eccl. Univers.*, L. 2, c. 8, n. 11-16. Barbosa's definitions are adopted almost *verbatim* by Mostazo, *De Causis Piis*, L. 5, c. 10, n. 2.

4 *De Oratoriis Dom.*, c. 3, n. 2.

5 *Bibliotheca*, v, s. v. "Oratorium," n. 2-4.

6 *De Oratoriis*, Pars I, c. 4.

7 *Jus Eccl. Univers.*, L. 2, c. 8, n. 11.

tum signum publici oratorii, et proinde supponit, quod jam sit publicum, non autem pertinet ad formam per quam constituitur publicum. Nam in tantum campana ordinatur ad convocandos populos, in quantum oratorium est omnium usui destinatum, atque adeo erectum, ut publicum."[8] Other elements that were stressed by some authors as necessary for a public oratory were a title and titular feast, a fixed and stable altar and the absence of an entrance into a private dwelling.[9] But these elements generally were considered as prescribed indeed, but not as absolutely essential, and this common opinion was later confirmed by various decisions of the Holy See.[10]

This distinction of oratories into public and private became of very great importance only after the Council of Trent demanded an Apostolic indult for the erection of private oratories.[11] But it was of some consequence even prior thereto, as a private oratory usually was more limited in its rights and privileges than a public oratory, even as the latter was more restricted therein than a church. These limitations, however, were determined by the local bishop at the time of the erection of each oratory rather than by various laws that were applicable to the different classes of oratories. In fact, as will be seen in the investigation of the pre-Tridentine legislation, the councils did not distinguish one class of oratories from the other. Nevertheless, it is certain that long before the Council of Trent some oratories were open to all the faithful and enjoyed extensive rights, while others were used only by a family or an individual and were subject to numerous limitations.

Having thus briefly considered the juridical division of oratories, it is expedient at least to indicate the various forms in which they were found, some of which arose

---

8 *Consultationes Canonicae,* I, Consult. 93, n. 24.

9 Cf. Ferraris, *Bibliotheca,* V, s. v. "Oratorium," n. 86 sq.; De Bonis, *De Oratoriis Pub.*, c. 12; Gasparri, *De SS. Eucharistia,* I, n. 190.

10 Cf. S. R. C., Nov. 12, 1831; D. A., 2682; for earlier decisions cf. Gattico, *De Oratoriis Dom.*, c. 3, n. 9 sq.

11 Consequently few authors before this Council define the two kinds of oratories.

only during the late Middle Ages. Besides the "Martyria" or Memorials of the Martyrs to which reference has been made, and the oratories erected in the monasteries and in episcopal residences which will come under discussion later, the following also are worthy of notice:[12]

1) *Cemetery or Mortuary Chapels*[13] were but a further extension of the "Martyria" and were erected on or near the common burial place of the faithful as the Christian counterpart to the pagan mausoleum.

2) *Chapels of Ease or Succursal Chapels* were erected in the larger parishes in sections remote from the parish church and were intended to render it easier for the faithful to attend divine services. At first the sacraments could not be administered in such chapels, but gradually this restriction was removed and such succursal chapels usually developed into filial churches and finally into independent parochial churches.

3) *Accessory Chapels* include ante-chapels, sub-chapels and side-chapels, that is, all chapels structurally forming part of a large church. They probably owe their origin to the ancient discipline—still retained in the Oriental Church—"Unum altare in una ecclesia" with its corollary "Una Missa in uno altari" which became difficult to observe when the practice arose of each priest offering his own daily Mass instead of concelebrating with the bishop. The accessory chapel offered but a partial solution to the difficulty and this ancient discipline soon ceased in the West where it probably never was general, though it certainly was observed in the Gallican and Ambrosian Rites.[14]

4) *Chantry Chapels* usually were accessory chapels that were erected and endowed solely for the celebration

12 For more extensive descriptions, cf. Smith-Cheetham, *Dictionary of Christian Antiquities*, I, s. v. "Chapel"; *Catholic Encyclopedia*, III, s. v. "Chapel"; Gasquet, *Parish Life in Mediaeval England*.

13 It is interesting to note that usage requires the term chapel to designate most of these forms of oratories.

14 For the controversy concerning this discipline in the West, cf. Bona, *Rer. Liturg.*, L. 1, c. 14, n. 3; Gasparri, *De SS. Eucharistia*, I, n. 287.

of Requiem Masses for some deceased person, generally its founder. They became very numerous in the Middle Ages and were in charge of special priests known as chantry priests.

5) *Chapels of Repose* owe their origin to an English mediæval custom. On Good Friday one of the Sacred Hosts that had been consecrated on Maundy Thursday and also the cross that had been used for the "Ecce lignum crucis" ceremony of Good Friday were placed in what was known as the Easter sepulchre or chapel of repose. On Easter morning they were brought back to the church in solemn procession, the whole ceremony symbolizing the burial of Christ's body and His glorious resurrection. In many churches this chapel of repose was only a temporary structure, while in others it not only was permanent and most elaborate, but also was the scene of the other liturgical functions proper to a public oratory. The term chapel of repose is now applied to the chapel in which the Blessed Sacrament is reserved from the Mass of Maundy Thursday to the Mass of the Presanctified on Good Friday.

6) *Ambassadors' Chapels* arose soon after the Reformation. The ambassadors of Catholic countries at a Protestant court were allowed to have chapels attached to their embassies even though the practice of the Catholic religion was proscribed by the penal law of the land. This was recognized as a right flowing from the immunity of diplomatic agents.[15]

7) *Royal Chapels* were those intended for the use of the royal family or any member thereof. In Catholic countries they differed but little from the oratories erected in the palaces of prelates and nobles. In countries where Catholicism was banned by law, any member of the royal family enjoyed the right of a chapel as a prerogative of royalty.

8) *Chapels in Hospitals and in other Charitable Institutions* throughout the early and Middle Ages in most

---

15 Wilson, *International Law*, c. 13, n. 78.

cases can be reduced to oratories in monasteries, as such institutions existed principally in conjunction with Religious houses; for as Thomassinus says: "Erant et in Monasteriis Xenodochia, erant et in Xenodochiis Monasteria, erant denique in utrisque oratoria."[16]

9) *Votive Chapels* may be taken as a generic term which includes most oratories not specifically enumerated above. They generally were erected through the devotion of private persons as a suitable way in which to commemorate some important event, to enshrine some precious relic, as a means of honoring some particular saint or mystery, of obtaining some special favor, etc. Among this class of oratories are to be found many of the famous European places of pilgrimage and also the very numerous wayside chapels which so eloquently testify to the thoroughly Catholic spirit that so long and so happily permeated Europe.

---

16 *Vet. et Nov. Disc.*, Pars I, L. 2, c. 93, n. 14.

PART II.

Pre-Code Legislation on Oratories.

CHAPTER V.

Legislation on Oratories Before the Council of Trent.

Article 1: Prefatory.

In considering the early legislation on oratories that which has been said concerning their origin and gradual development must be remembered. It is almost unnecessary to add that until the late Middle Ages little more than isolated canons of particular councils will be found which have a direct bearing on oratories. General enactments, whether papal or conciliar, were devoted almost exclusively to matters of a dogmatic nature or to the more flagrant disciplinary abuses. It is evidently beyond the scope of this treatise to give all the particular legislation that was enacted concerning oratories—nor will that be necessary; a few councils will be cited from the different ages and from various localities, and from their more or less similar laws the general trend of the legislation on oratories can be gaged with sufficient accuracy. Practically all of the councils that will be cited were concerned with one or several of the following questions:

1) May an oratory or any other place of worship be erected on private authority? 2) Must the holy Sacrifice be offered only in dedicated churches or may it be offered also in oratories and in other places? 3) Is the permission of the bishop required for offering Mass in oratories? 4) May any of the sacraments be administered in an oratory? 5) What are the relations of an oratory to the parish church in whose territory it is situated? 6) What restrictions is an oratory subject to

relative to the time and kind of divine services that may be performed in it? 7) Should an oratory be dedicated? 8) Does it enjoy ecclesiastical immunity and especially the right of asylum?

No council legislated on all of these matters, and such as were referred to often were treated only in as far as they were connected with some other matter that was primarily under consideration. The difficulty of understanding this legislation becomes all the greater in view of the fact that the councils did not expressly distinguish public from private oratories, nor the private oratories in which the holy Sacrifice could be offered from those which were intended merely as places of prayer. If to these difficulties we add that the terms "ecclesia" and "oratorium" were still used interchangeably, at least at times, and that the laws of the particular councils despite their general similarity nevertheless did vary considerably in different localities, it becomes evident that it is impossible to give the exact answer to all of the above questions from the legislation of any particular century. Nevertheless a brief survey of these councils will be useful, as from them can best be seen the gradual development in the legislation on oratories throughout the centuries, a legislation that was to receive its clearest and most precise expression in the Code.

The legislation on oratories before the Council of Trent will be treated here in three articles under the captions: 1) The erection of oratories. 2) Divine services in oratories. 3) Dedication and ecclesiastical immunity of oratories. A summary of the status of oratories before the Council of Trent then will be added.

Article 2: The Erection of Oratories.

It may be well to emphasize at once that whatever restrictions were placed on the erection of oratories had reference to oratories in which divine services were to be held, not to such as were intended and used only as places of prayer. For man has a natural right of praying to God in any and every place, and consequently, also the lesser right of reserving some place in his home in which to offer his prayers and hold the family devotions. This right was recognized at all times [1] and was expressly stated in c. 3 of the Council of Orleans [2] (held in 511) which is cited by Gratian as c. 33, D. 1, *de cons.*: "Unicuique fidelium licet in domo sua oratorium habere et ibi orare."[3] Hence an oratory in this restricted meaning of a place reserved for prayer alone is patently not included in the legislation on the erection of an oratory, but only those oratories were affected which were used for liturgical services. This having been premised, the legislation itself will be considered.

The Council of Gangra (324 or 330) in c. 6 states: "Si quis extra ecclesiam seorsum conventus celebrat, et despiciens ecclesiam, ea, quae sunt ecclesiae, voluerit usurpare, non conveniente presbytero juxta decretum episcopi, anathema sit." [4] This canon is cited by some authors as the earliest extant law on oratories in the form of a prohibition—indirect and by implication—of their erection. This interpretation, however, seems beyond that which the wording of the canon warrants. The Council of Gangra in this canon, and also in c. 20 [5] which further develops the phrase, "despiciens ecclesiam," seems to be opposing only such gatherings as were of a schismatic or heretical character. C. 5 of the Council of Antioch (340) deals with the same matter in clearer terms: "Si quis presbyter vel diaconus proprio contempto episcopo, ab ecclesia seipsum segregaverit, et privatim congregationem effecerit, et altare erexerit, et episcopo accersente non obedierit, is omnino deponatur."[6]

Though the above canons thus easily can be eliminated, the next century offered a law of a General Council which

---

1 Cf. Gattico, *De Oratoriis Dom.*, c. 3, n. 16.
2 Mansi, VIII, 364.
3 This right is asserted also in the "Corpus Juris Civilis" of Justinian, Nov. 58.
4 Mansi, II, 1106.
5 Mansi, II, 1112.
6 Mansi, II, 1310.

expressly prohibited the erection of oratories unless the permission of the bishop had been obtained. The law in question is c. 4 of the Council of Chalcedon (451): "Quoniam quidam sub protextu habitu monachi ecclesias, et conventus, et res communes disturpant, civitates circumeuntes indiscrete, necnon et monasteria sibi constituere studentes, placuit, ut nullum eorum usquam aedificare liceat, neque monasterium constituere, neque oratorium absque civitatis episcopi voluntate."[7] This canon definitely determined that for the erection of an oratory (or of a monastery) the permission of the bishop was necessary; and as it was a canon of a General Council, this became the law for the universal Church. Nor can the objection be urged in virtue of the introductory clauses that the Council of Chalcedon was opposing abuses somewhat similar to those referred to above in the Councils of Gangra and Antioch, and that therefore it likewise was placing a restriction only on oratories that would be erected by those who were a disturbing element in the Church. For such an objection has no force in view of the nature as well as of the wording of the respective canons. The canons of the Councils of Gangra and Antioch were penal; they named an offense and designated its penalty. These canons, therefore, were to be applied only to those who were guilty of the offense in question, namely, of despising the Church, disobeying its lawfully constituted authority, holding seditious or schismatic gatherings, etc. The canon of the Council of Chalcedon, however, was a positive ordinance demanding the authorization of the bishop for the erection of an oratory or of a monastery. In the preamble the canon indeed mentions the abuses which occasioned the law, but the statute itself, "Placuit ut nullum, etc.," is general and is not limited to the abuses which the preamble assigns as the reason for the law.

If the correctness of this interpretation needs any further proof, an investigation of the subsequent legislation will afford it. It is true that until the Twelfth Century

---

7 Mansi, VII, 394.

few if any councils expressly and formally restate this law of the Council of Chalcedon; nevertheless they do state that holy Mass could not be offered in oratories without the bishop's permission. This is equivalent in its results to stating that the bishop's permission was required for the erection of an oratory for offering the holy Sacrifice and thus is indirectly restating the law of the Council of Chalcedon. For it is evident when the Council of Chalcedon demanded episcopal permission for the erection of an oratory it meant one in which divine services were to be offered, as the erection or possession of an oratory which was to be used merely as a place of prayer never was forbidden. To express the same truth from a different viewpoint, one might say that these councils demanded the bishop's permission for changing an oratory from a mere place of prayer to an oratory in which Mass was to be offered, while the Council of Chalcedon demanded the bishop's permission for erecting an oratory in which Mass was to be offered without considering the question whether the oratory was or was not already in existence as a mere place of prayer.

As these councils that demanded the bishop's permission for offering the holy Sacrifice will be referred to in the next article, they will be omitted here. Hence only the legislation of the councils of the late Middle Ages whose prohibition is identical with that of the Council of Chalcedon in form as well as in result need yet be considered. Without pretending to offer the legislation of all of these councils, the following are presented as examples of the general trend and form of the legislation that was then enacted on this subject: Council of London (held in 1102 under St. Anselm), c. 15: "Ne novae cappellae fiant sine consensu episcopi;"[8] Council of London (held in 1138 under Albert, Cardinal Legate and Bishop of Ostia), c. 12: "Apostolica auctoritate prohibemus, ne quis absque licentia episcopi sui in possessione sua ecclesiam vel oratorium constituat;"[9] Synod

[8] Mansi, XX, 1151.
[9] Mansi, XXI, 513.

of Exeter (1287), c. 9: "Non liceat cuiquam ecclesiam vel cappellam de novo construere absque episcopi sui licentia speciali;"[10] Council of Sens (1528), c. 13: "Inhibemus cappellas de novo erigi, construi, etiam omnino dirutas reaedificari, sine dioecesanorum licentia et permissione.'"[11] Finally, Gratian's manner of citing c. 4 of the Council of Chalcedon is worthy of quotation: "Placuit neminem aut aedificare aut construere monasteria aut oratorii domum sine conscientia ipsius civitatis episcopi.'"[12] From these and other canons that could be cited as reflecting the law of the Council of Chalcedon, confirmatory arguments are found which clearly indicate that throughout the centuries subsequent to the Council of Chalcedon the bishop's permission was required for the erection of all oratories that were used for the celebration of holy Mass.

It is true that most Religious erected the oratories in their monasteries without obtaining the permission of the bishop; this, however, was due to the fact that they were exempt from the observance of the existing law in virtue of particular privileges. At the time of the Council of Trent practically all the Religious Orders [13] had long since obtained such privileges [14] either by direct concession of the Holy See or in virtue of the so-called communication of privileges. However, it must be observed that these privileges of Regulars were restricted to their own exempt territory and could not be exercised elsewhere as was declared by Alexander IV whose decree was incorporated in the "Liber Sextus" of Boniface VIII: "Auctoritate Sedis Apostolicae statuimus quod oratoria vel cappellas in locis non exemptis sine

---

10 Mansi, XXIV, 798.

11 Mansi, XXXII, 1189.

12 C. 10; C. XVIII, q. 2.

13 Cf. Pasqualigo, *De Sacrificio*, I, Quaest. 484; Petra, *Commentaria ad Constitutiones Apostolicas*, I, *In Const. 8 Honorii III*, n. 35; Van Gameren, *De Oratoriis*, Pars II, c. 2, art. 2.

14 Many had obtained the even more extensive privilege of a portable altar in virtue of which they could offer Mass even outside of oratories in any decent place; cf. c. 30, X, *de privilegiis*, V, 33.

dioecesanorum locorum ipsorum licentia exempti construere non praesumant.''[15]

Article 3: Divine Services in Oratories.

In the previous article the permission of the bishop was shown to be necessary for the erection of an oratory; this permission included or implied also the permission of having the holy Sacrifice celebrated in that oratory. This right, however, frequently was usurped and other abuses perpetrated by the possessors of oratories that had been erected without episcopal permission. Hence various councils enacted laws prohibiting the celebration of Mass outside of churches. Some of these laws contained the clause: ''Unless the permission of the bishop had been obtained;'' others were absolute and unrestricted. However, it is certain that even where this clause was not expressly stated, it nevertheless was implied and understood. If that had not been the case, the many laws that demanded episcopal permission for the erection of oratories would have had no *raison d'être.* For, as was shown, the faithful were absolutely free to erect oratories which were to be used merely as places of prayer, and therefore the oratories for whose erection the bishop's permission was required must have possessed additional privileges, the most important of which was the right of being used for the celebration of Mass. These facts must be borne in mind in considering the legislation that was passed concerning the celebration of divine services, for from some of the laws one might be led falsely to conclude that divine services could be held only in consecrated churches.

For the sake of clearness the legislation in this article will be presented in three sections and will refer to: 1) The celebration of Mass in oratories.[16] 2) Limitations as to the time for offering Mass. 3) The administration of the sacraments.

---

[15] C. 4, *de privilegiis,* V. 7, in VI; cf. also c. 14, X, *de privilegiis,* V, 33.

[16] That a special section is devoted to this subject (even though it already has been treated, at least indirectly, in the previous article) is due to its great importance and to the very nature of the laws that were enacted.

Section 1: The Celebration of Mass in Oratories.

The earliest law that can be cited as pertinent to this subject is c. 58 of the Council of Laodicea (held about 350 or 380) which enacted: "Quod non oporteat in domibus oblationes celebrari ab episcopis vel presbyteris."[17] This canon is quite general and seems opposed to the thesis that Mass could be offered in oratories provided the permission of the bishop had been obtained. Various attempts have been made to reconcile this canon with the known fact that Mass was celebrated lawfully in some oratories. Gattico[18] asserts that this canon was intended as a weapon to be used against the Eustachians rather than as a general prohibition of celebrating Mass outside of churches. Thomassinus[19] says that the canon of the Council of Laodicea must be understood as referring to houses situated in cities that contained churches, not to houses in rural districts where for a long time there were no churches. Another plausible explanation is that the canon of the Council of Laodicea forbade the celebration of Mass in ordinary homes or oratories, but not in those oratories that had been given this right by the bishop.

However, even if these and other explanations be rejected, and it be maintained that this canon absolutely prohibited Mass in oratories, it must be remembered that this is a canon of one particular council. Even granting that a few other canons of similar doubtful tenor are found in different centuries, they are more than counterbalanced by the legislation of other councils which expressly state that Mass could be offered in oratories with the bishop's permission. For the claim is not advanced that the legislation was unanimous in this matter; all that is maintained is that it was sufficiently uniform to warrant the assertion that as a general rule holy Mass could be offered with the bishop's permission. To further substantiate this proposition, a number of

---

17 Mansi, II, 582.

18 *De Oratoriis Dom.*, c. 4, n. 9.

19 *Vet. et Nov. Disc.*, Pars I, L. 2, c. 92, n. 8-9.

laws will be cited, only a few words of comment occasionally being added.

The Council of Carthage (390), c. 9: "Quisquis presbyter inconsulto episcopo agenda in quolibet loco voluerit celebrare, ipse honori suo contrarius existit."[20] This canon negatively implies that with the permission of the bishop a priest could offer Mass "in quolibet loco" and therefore in an oratory.[21]

The IV Council of Orleans (541), c. 7: "Ut in oratoriis domini praediorum minime contra votum episcopi, ad quem territorii ipsius privilegium noscitur pertinere, peregrinos clericos intromittant." [22] The reason for admitting these clerics evidently was for the purpose of celebrating Mass, as their merely passive presence in such oratories certainly would not require the permission of the bishop.

The Council of Trullo (692), c. 31: "Clericos qui in oratoriis, quae sunt intra domos, sacra faciunt . . . hoc illius loci episcopi sententia facere debere decernimus."[23]

Pope Zachary (741) in his "Responsa ad Pipinum et Francorum Episcopos de Variis Capitulis Francorum," n. 15: "Oratorium quod laici in suis proprietatibus construunt, absque missis publicis solemniter consecrabitur; . . . et si missa ibi facere maluerint, ab episcopo presbyterum postulandum."[24]

The Council of Mayence (813), c. 26: "Ut presbyteris per monasteria puellarum opportuno tempore liceat missarum sollemnia celebrare, et iterum ad proprias ecclesias redire."[25] This is an example of the laws confirming the privilege of Religious of having the holy Sacrifice offered in the oratories of their monasteries.

The Synod of Rome (under Leo IV in 853), c. 21: "Oratorium canonice constructum a dominio construc-

---

20 Mansi, III, 695.

21 Cf. *Corpus Juris Civilis Justiniani,* Nov. 58 and 67.

22 Mansi, IX, 114. Cf. also c. 14 of the Council of Chalons sur-Saone (650); Mansi, X, 1192.

23 Mansi, XI, 955.

24 Mansi, XII, 331.

25 Mansi, XIV, 72.

toris invite non auferatur, liceatque id illi presbytero cui voluerit pro sacro officio . . . cum consensu episcopi commendare."[26]

The Council of Mainz (888), c. 9: "Missarum solemnia non ubique, sed in locis ab episcopo consecratis, vel ubi permiserit, celebranda esse censemus."[27]

The Laws for the Priests of Northumbria (950), c. 13: "Si presbyter in non consecratis aedibus missam celebret, solvat XII oras."[28] Even canons of this nature which prohibited Mass in non-consecrated places are not contrary to our thesis, as the custom of consecrating oratories was in vogue for centuries.

The Council of Clermont-Ferrand (1095), c. 18: "Ut nullus presbyter cappellanus alicuius laici esse possit absque concessione sui episcopi."[29] The canon states that the consent of the bishop was necessary for the appointment of the chaplain; but the principal duty of a chaplain was to offer the holy Sacrifice in a chapel.

The Council of Cologne (1280), c. 15: "Statuimus ut nullus sacerdos in cappella audeat celebrare sine nostra licentia, quantumcumque a patronis ad hoc licentientur vel etiam permittantur."[30]

The Synod of Autun (1301), c. 7: "Prohibemus etiam ne aliqui in locis privatis absque licentia praelati loci illius praesumat divina celebrare."[31]

The Council of London (1321), c. 6: "Decrevimus quemcunque in oratoriis, cappellis, aut domibus, seu in loco minime dedicato Missarum solemnia celebrare diœcesani non obtenta licentia, suspensionem a Divinorum celebratione ipso facto per mensem incurrere."[32]

To the above canons some of those quoted in the next section could be added here also; but sufficient texts have been cited to prove that with the bishop's permission

---

26 Mansi, XIV, 1006.
27 Mansi, XVIII A, 67.
28 Wilkins, *Concilia Magnae Britanniae,* I, 219.
29 Mansi, XX, 817.
30 Mansi, XXIV, 360.
31 Mansi, XXXII, 322.
32 Mansi, XXV, 676.

Mass could be offered in oratories. The proof of this proposition has been developed at considerable length because of its very great importance, the right to the celebration of Mass being to a large extent the basis of and the prerequisite for the other privileges that were granted to oratories.

Section 2: Limitations as to the Time for Offering Mass.

Already in the early Church the right of offering holy Mass in oratories was restricted by various laws forbidding the exercise of this right on certain feast days. The purpose of such legislation evidently was—as some of the laws expressly stated—to secure the attendance of all the faithful in their own parish churches at least occasionally during the year. The days on which Mass could be offered only in episcopal or parish churches were enumerated somewhat differently by nearly every council that legislated on the subject; but the underlying principle was preserved that on the more important feasts—whichever they may have been considered to be—Mass should not be celebrated in the oratories. As examples of these restrictive laws the following may be cited:

The Council of Agde (506), c. 21: "Si quis extra parochias, in quibus legitimus est ordinariusque conventus, oratorium in agro habere voluerit; reliquis festivitatibus, ut ibi missas teneat propter fatigationem familiae, justa ordinatione permittimus. Pascha vero, Natale Domini, Epiphania, Ascensionem Domini, Pentecostem, et Natalem S. Joannis Baptistae, vel si qui maximi dies in festivitatibus habentur, non nisi in civitatibus aut in parochiis teneant. Clerici vero, si qui in festivitatibus habentur, quas supra diximus, in oratoriis, nisi jubente aut permittente episcopo, missas facere aut tenere voluerint, a communione pellantur."[33] This is probably the earliest law on the subject; it is of interest to note that it clearly states that even on these specified days the bishop could allow Mass in the oratories. The Council of Orleans (511) forbade Mass in oratories on Christmas, Easter

---

33 Mansi, VIII, 328.

and during Lent;[34] The Council of Clermont in Auvergne (535) on Christmas, Easter, Pentecost and the other principal feast days—"Principales reliquae solemnitates."[35] These councils sufficiently illustrate the point under discussion and therefore it is not necessary to refer to any others; but c. 33 of the Council of Angers (1365) contains such an unusual enumeration of the days on which it prohibited Mass in oratories that it is worthy of citation if only as a curiosity: "Statuimus quod quotiescumque per aliquem episcopum alicui nobili vel personae saeculari celebrandi divina officia in domibus suis vel cappellis licentiam contigerit impartiri, quod illae sex dies, scilicet prima dies Dominica in Adventu Domini, Dominica post Epiphaniam, prima Dominica in Quadragesima, Dominica in Passione Domini, Dominica post Pentecostem Domini, Dominica post festum Assumptionis B. V. Mariae, a concessione generali sint exceptae, in quibus sex dies per nullum poterit in dictis domibus seu cappellis celebrari."[36]

In the oratories of Religious, however, Mass could be offered even on the days when it was prohibited in other oratories lest the Religious be obliged to leave their monasteries to attend the festive celebrations in the parish churches. The faithful, taking advantage of this right of the Religious, gradually began to frequent their oratories also on these days. Hence various councils during the Middle Ages endeavored to counteract this practice by commanding the faithful to attend Mass in their own parochial church on all Sundays and solemn feast days, and by demanding that the Religious either do not admit the laity to divine services on these days, or that they conduct them at an hour which would not interfere with the faithful attending Mass in their own parish church. Thus the Council of Arles (1260) in c. 15 declared: "Districtius inhibemus ne religiosi in ecclesiis suis aut cappellis laicos diebus Dominicis et solemnitati-

---

34 C. 25; Mansi, VIII, 355.
35 C. 15; Mansi, VIII, 862.
36 Mansi, XXVI, 444.

bus praecipuis recipiant ad Divina; nec horis illis, in suis locis populo publice praedicent, quibus in parochiis Missarum solemnia celebrantur;"[37] and the Council of Buda-Veszprem (1279) in c. 33: "Praecipimus ut parochiani singulis diebus Dominicis et festivis ad Missam vadant ad suas parochiales ecclesias, ibique divina officia audiant: nec ipsi parochiani, relicta sua parochiali ecclesia ad alias cujuscumque sint ordinis, religionis, aut status, sive sint parochiales ecclesiae sive non ad audiendam Missam praesumant accedere."[38]

That the faithful were not at liberty to attend Mass in the oratories even of Religious on Sundays and feast days, but were obliged to do so in their parish churches is expressly stated in a decree of Sixtus IV to the clergy of Germany in 1478: "Mandamus . . . . quod Fratres Mendicantes non praedicent, populos parochianos non teneri audire missam in eorum parochiis diebus festivis et dominicis, *quum jure sit cautum*, illis diebus parochianos teneri audire missam in eorum parochiali ecclesia."[39] The same Pontiff, however, immediately adds: "Nisi forsan ex honesta causa ab ipsa ecclesia se absentarent," which indicates that the above general obligation admitted of exceptions.

Section 3: *The Administration of Sacraments in Oratories.*

Except in the primitive Church the administration of Baptism was enumerated among the strictly parochial[40] functions and, therefore, was prohibited in oratories.[41] On this subject Gattico writes: "Alterum parochorum

---

37 Mansi, XXIII, 1010.

38 Mansi, XXIV, 285. Similar though less rigorous laws are found already in the eighth century; e.g., cf. c. 46 of the Capitularies of Theodulf, Bishop of Orleans; Mansi, XIII, 1006.

39 C. 2, *de treuga et pace*, I, 9, in Extravag. com.

40 Even though it be admitted that parish churches strictly so-called became general only at the beginning of the Middle Ages, still it is certain that the parochial rights were reserved even prior thereto to the principal churches.

41 Baluzius in his "Notae ad Capitularia Regum Francorum," s. v. "Ecclesiae Baptismales" (Mansi, XVIII bis, 1063 sq.), proves that during the early centuries not even all parish churches enjoyed the right of a baptismal font.

jus, quod in Baptismatis administratione consistit, a nullo invadi posse sine Canonum despectu exploratissimum penitus est. Revera catechumenos baptizare, et per Baptismum intra Ovile Ecclesiae recipere munus pastorum est."[42] Of the many canons that could be cited in confirmation of this proposition, the following are selected because of their brevity and clearness.

The Council of Trullo (692), c. 59: "In aede oratoria baptismus nequaquam peragatur: sed qui illuminatione ab omnibus sordibus aliena digni habendi sunt, ad catholicas ecclesias accedant, et hoc illic munere perfruatur."[43] Pope Zachary (741) in his "Responsa ad Pipinum et Francorum Episcopos de Variis Capitulis Francorum," n. 15: "Oratorium quod laici in suis proprietatibus construunt, absque missis publicis solemniter consecrabitur, ita ut in eodem loco, nec futuris temporibus baptisteria construantur."[44] Pope Zachary is here quoting almost verbatim the words of Pope Gregory the Great (590-604) in a particular response to a certain Bishop Passivus.[45] The Council of Meaux (845), c. 48: "Ut nemo presbyterorum baptizare praesumat, nisi in vicis et ecclesiis baptismalibus, nisi causa aegritudinis vel certae necessitatis."[46] Finally, the following decree of Clement V, incorporated in the "Clementinae," was obligatory for the whole Church: "Prohibemus ne quis in aulis vel cameris aut aliis privatis domibus, sed duntaxat in ecclesiis, in quibus sunt ad hoc fontes specialiter deputati, aliquos, (nisi regum vel principum, quibus valeat in hoc casu deferri, liberi exstiterint, aut talis necessitas emerserit, propter quam nequeat ad ecclesiam absque periculo propter hoc accessus haberi,) audeat baptizare."[47]

The sacrament of Confirmation was administered almost exclusively in the parish church, and Holy Orders

---

42 *De Oratoriis Dom.*, c. 28, n. 3.
43 Mansi, XI, 970.
44 Mansi, XII, 331.
45 L. VII, Pars II, ep. 71; Mansi, X, 161.
46 Mansi, XIV, 830.
47 C. un., *de Baptismo et ejus effectu*, III, 15, in Clem.

in the cathedral church. If any exceptions were made in favor of oratories—and none are evident from the legislation —they caused no trouble, as the administration of these sacraments presupposed the presence of the bishop who would give the necessary permission if the circumstances warranted the administration of either sacrament in an oratory. It is true that in the Oriental Church Confirmation was administered by the priest immediately after Baptism;[48] but the Council of Trullo and subsequent councils forbade the administration of Baptism in oratories, and these prohibitions included or implied also the administration of Confirmation in oratories.

The celebration of Matrimony in oratories was a privilege seldom conceded, and when given usually was in favor of royal chapels only.[49] Marriage was to take place in the church: "Nuptiae fieri debent in ecclesia coram populo;"[50] and the church in question was the parish church: "Prius conveniendus est sacerdos in cuius parochia nuptiae fieri debent in ecclesia."[51] On this subject some councils expressly referred to oratories and forbade the celebration of Matrimony therein; thus the Council of Exeter (1287), c. 9: "Nec in ipsis (cappellis) nuptiae celebrentur;"[52] and the Council of Tortosa (1429), c. 7: "Neque etiam Missa pro nuptiis . . . vel novinuptiis in domibus vel cappellis celebretur."[53] The banns, likewise, were to be proclaimed (not in oratories, but) in churches as was decreed by the IV General Council of the Lateran (1215), c. 51: "Statuimus ut cum matrimonia fuerint contrahenda, in ecclesiis per presbyteros publice proponantur."[54]

In the administration of the sacrament of Penance the jurisdiction of the minister rather than the lawfulness

48 Cf. Benedict XIV, *De Synodo Dioecesana*, L. 7, c. 9.

49 Cf. Martene, *De Antiquis Ecclesiae Ritibus*, L. 1, c. 9, art. 2, n. 4.

50 *Capitularia Regum Francorum*, L. VII, c. 179; Mansi, XVII bis, 1062.

51 *Canones Isaac, Episcopi Lingonensis*, (Langres) Tit. 5, c. 6; Mansi, XVII bis, 1263.

52 Mansi, XXIV, 798.

53 Mansi, XXVIII, 1148.

54 Mansi, XXII, 1038.

of the place of ministration was primarily the subject of legislation. In the very early Church the bishop alone was the ordinary and usual minister of this sacrament.[55] As the number of the faithful increased, the hearing of confessions became one of the ordinary duties of priests as it was impossible for the bishops to give sacramental absolution to all who sought it. Although in some places special priest penitentiaries—often monks—were entrusted with this office,[56] it more generally became the right and duty of the parish priest, the reason for this being as c. 8 of the Synodal Statutes of Rheims, (639) stated "Huius (pastoris) enim interest ovem recognoscere, pro qua suam animam foenerat Domino."[57] Thus at a very early date the administration of Penance began to assume to some extent the nature of a parochial right and as such was administered in the parish church. But the practice of empowering other priests, especially Religious, to hear confessions continued. That they at least occasionally exercised this power in oratories to which the faithful had access cannot be questioned.[58] This practice became more prevalent after the institution of the great Orders of St. Francis and St. Dominic which were given very liberal powers of administering this and other sacraments by various pontiffs.[59]

But apart from these privileges of Religious, the ordinary place for administering the sacrament of Penance was the church, and only in cases of necessity or in virtue of a special privilege was it administered elsewhere as was expressly stated by the Synodal Constitutions of the diocese of Valencia (1255), c. *de confessione*: "Extra ecclesiam nullus audiat confessiones, nisi in necessitate magna aut infirmitate;"[60] and by c. 8 of the Synod

55 Cf. Thomassinus, *Vet. et Nov. Disc.*, Pars I, L. 2, c. 23, n. 2; Van Espen, *Jus Eccl. Univers.*, Pars II, Sect. 1, Tit. 6, c. 6; Martene, *De Antiquis Ecclesiae Ritibus*, L. 1, Pars II, c. 6, art. 6, n. 2.

56 Cf. Martene, *l. c.*, n. 3.

57 Mansi, X, 598.

58 Cf. Gattico, *De Oratoriis Dom.*, c. 3, n. 6.

59 Cf. e.g., c. 1, *de privilegiis*, V, 7, in Extravag. com., and c. 2, *de sepulturis*, III, 7, in Clem.

60 Mansi, XXIII, 888.

of Cologne (1280): "Ad confessionem audiendam aptum locum in ecclesia sibi eligant sacerdotes. In locis autem obscuris non audiant confessiones, nec extra ecclesiam, nisi in magna necessitate aut infirmitate."[61] These canons represent and reflect what was the general practice in the Church and the departures from it can be explained as resulting from local custom or particular privilege.

That the annual obligatory confession was reserved to the proper pastor and hence could not be heard by the chaplains of oratories was decreed by canon 21 of the IV General Council of the Lateran (1215): "Omnis utriusque sexus fidelis, postquam ad annos discretionis pervenerit, omnia sua peccata confiteatur fideliter, saltem semel in anno, proprio sacerdoti . . . suscipiens reverenter ad minus in Pascha Eucharistiae sacramentum; . . . alioquin et vivens ab ingressu ecclesiae arceatur, et moriens Christiana careat sepultura. Si quis autem alieno sacerdoti voluerit justa de causa sua confiteri peccata, licentiam prius postulet et obtineat a proprio sacerdote, cum aliter ille ipse non possit solvere vel ligare."[62] Although made universal law only in the Thirteenth Century, the reservation of the obligatory confession to pastors had been in force in virtue of particular laws for centuries. Thus already the Synodal Statutes of Rheims (639), c. 8 had decreed: "Nemo tempore quadragesimae poenitentium confessiones audiat praeter pastorem."[63] The Lateran decree was repeated with special reference to Religious by Sixtus IV in 1478;[64] but in regard to the oratories of Religious institutions it must be remembered that the clergy in charge thereof were the "sacerdotes proprii" at least of the Religious residing there who, therefore, certainly could fulfil this duty in their own oratories and to their own chaplains.

Considerable difficulty is encountered in attempting to determine the rights of oratories in the administration

---

61 Mansi, XXIV, 353.
62 Mansi, XXII, 1007.
63 Mansi, X, 598.
64 C. 2, *de treuga et pace*, I, 9, in Extravag. com.

of Holy Communion during the centuries under consideration. The mere fact that holy Mass could be offered did not necessarily include the right of administering Holy Communion there.[65] It is true that in the early Church as a general rule those who attended Mass also received Holy Communion,[66] no matter where the Mass was celebrated.[67] Nevertheless, as the oratories for offering Mass became more numerous and the danger of abuses greater, the administration of Holy Communion in oratories was quite generally forbidden unless special permission had been obtained from the bishop. This is evident from the laws that forbade the administration of any of the sacraments in oratories, as for example, c. 9 of the Synod of Exeter (1287): "Inhibemus ne in cappellis parochianis matricis ecclesiae nec aliis quibuscumque sacramenta ministrentur, nisi aliquibus aliis amplius fuerit indultum;"[68] and also from the laws that expressly forbade the distribution of Holy Communion in oratories, as did c. 7 of the Council of Tortosa (1429): "Statuimus quod nemini sano per privatos domos vel cappellas sacramentum Eucharistiae ministrentur, sed ipsis sanis in ecclesiis, et certis locis ad hoc deputatis, vel etiam specialiter deputandis."[69] These two canons are selected because even though they prohibit the distribution of Holy Communion in oratories they likewise indicate that this right could be and at times was conceded.

No apodictic statement can be made as to the frequency or extent of the concession of this right. However, it seems certain that in the oratories in private homes the right of receiving Holy Communion was granted only to the members of the household, and often not even to them. Oratories that served as succursal chapels for the large

65 Cf. Pasqualigo, *De Sacrificio*, I, Quaest. 644.

66 Cf. Cavalieri, *Opera Liturgica*, V, c. 24, n. 3.

67 In fact, during the persecutions the faithful frequently reserved the Blessed Sacrament in their homes and administered Holy Communion to themselves when unable to attend Mass; cf. Martene, *De Antiquis Ecclesiae Ritibus*, L. 1, Pars I, c. 5, art. 1, n. 1-3.

68 Mansi, XXIV, 799.

69 Mansi, XXVIII, 1148.

parishes usually were granted the same rights of administering Holy Communion as the parish churches themselves.[70] In oratories of Religious it is evident that the Religious themselves could receive Holy Communion. But until almost the Thirteenth Century the laity usually were not allowed to frequent many of these oratories except on special occasions and consequently did not receive Holy Communion there.[71] With the institution of the great Mendicant Orders, however, a conventual church or an oratory to which the faithful had free access and in which the sacraments of Penance and Holy Eucharist could be administered became part of every monastery by papal privilege.

The danger that these privileges of the Religious would prove an occasion for the faithful neglecting their parish churches was so imminent that various laws were enacted to safeguard the parish churches. Among these were the laws that demanded the permission of the pastor when any one else administered Holy Communion to a member of his flock. Thus c. 20 of the Synod of Chichester (1289) stated: "Nullus presbyterorum, alienum parochianum ad communionem corporis Christi praesumat admittere, sine licentia proprii sacerdotis." [72] And the next century affords a universal law to the same effect in the Clementine Decretals: "Religiosi, qui clericis aut laicis sacramentum (unctionis extremae vel) eucharistiae ministrare, (matrimoniave solemnizare,) non habita super his parochialis presbyteri licentia speciali . . . excommunicationis incurrant sententiam ipso facto, per sedem apostolicam duntaxat absolvendi. . . . Sane, religiosis illis, quibus est ab apostolica sede concessum, ut familiaribus suis domesticis, aut pauperibus, in hospitalibus suis degentibus, sacramenta possint ecclesiastica ministrare, nullum ex praemissis volumus quoad hoc praejudicium generari." [73]

---

70 But even in these succursal chapels the right of distributing Holy Communion during the Easter season usually was withheld.

71 Cf. Gattico, *De Oratoriis Dom.*, c. 8, n. 7-18.

72 Mansi, XXIV, 20.

73 C. 1, *de privilegiis,* V, 7, in Clem.

Only gradually was the necessity of obtaining this permission of the pastor restricted to the Easter Communion. This more lenient interpretation of the decree of Pope Clement V was based on the tacit consent of the Holy See, the passive acquiescence of pastors and local custom; after the Council of Trent it was expressly acknowledged by the popes in the new privileges which they granted to different Religious Orders. The decree of the Council of the Lateran (quoted above) concerning the Easter Communion, however, retained its original force not only to the Council of Trent, but even to the time of the promulgation of the Code; hence in no oratory could Easter Communion be distributed unless the permission of the pastor had been obtained.

Article 4: Dedication and Ecclesiastical Immunity of Oratories.

The question of the dedication of oratories during the centuries under discussion is quite complicated, not only because it is not at all evident at what time the distinction between the consecration and the blessing of sacred places was first instituted,[74] but also because several entirely different practices regarding the dedication of oratories can be traced prior to the Council of Trent. In a general way the following statements seem substantiated by an investigation of the legislation on the subject and of its commentators.

1) During the first three centuries, because of the severity of the persecutions, very few places of worship were dedicated, the Christians worshipping wherever they could. 2) After the persecutions the practice was observed of dedicating all places of worship in which the holy Sacrifice was offered. This is evident from the many laws that prohibited the celebration of Mass outside of consecrated places: "Ut in domibus ab episcopo non consecratis nemo Missam quacunque necessitate cele-

---

74 Cf. De Bonis, *De Oratoriis Pub.*, n. 164.

bret."[75] But as Mass was offered lawfully in some oratories they must have been consecrated. 3) The consecration of all sacred places used for the holy Sacrifice continued until about the Tenth Century when the practice arose of allowing Mass to be offered in oratories with the permission of the bishop even though they had not been consecrated: "Missarum solemnia non ubique, sed in locis ab episcopo consecratis, *vel ubi permiserit*, celebranda esse censemus."[76] Various reasons[77] have been assigned for this relaxation of the long existing discipline, the most practical one being that by this time the number of churches and oratories was increasing so rapidly that it was too great a burden for the bishop to consecrate (and when necessary, to reconcile) all of them. Hence, at least the less important oratories now frequently were dedicated by the simpler rite of benediction (by a priest) or solely by the offering of holy Mass. 4) But even during the succeeding centuries many oratories were consecrated, no uniform practice in this matter being observed in the universal Church.

Since the consecration of a sacred place implied its perpetual dedication to God's service—"Semel Deo dedicatum non est ad usus humanos ulterius transferendum"[78]—and as there was danger that the oratories erected on the estates of the laity might in the course of time be used for profane purposes, the General[79] Council of Constance (1416) forbade their consecration unless erected and endowed as ecclesiastical benefices: "Mandat haec Synodus quod Episcopi amplius cappellas . . . extra monasteria et conventus religiosorum sita nullatenus consecrent, nisi prius hujusmodi cappellae sint suf-

---

[75] Capitularies of Herardus, Archbishop of Tours (858), c. 34; Mansi, XVII bis, 1287; cf. also Council of Paris (829), c. 47 (Mansi, XIV, 566); First Capitularies of Charlemagne (769), c. 14 (Mansi, XVII bis, 192); Response of Pope Zachary (741), n. 15 (Mansi, XII, 331); Council of Braga (572), c. 5 (Mansi, IX, 839); Nov. 67, c. 1 of Justinian, etc.

[76] Council of Mainz (888), c. 9; Mansi, XVIII A, 67.

[77] Cf. Gattico, *De Oratoriis Dom.*, c. 12, n. 14; De Bonis, *De Oratoriis Pub.*, n. 164.

[78] R. J. 51 in VI.

[79] Only the late sessions of this Council are recognized as oecumenical.

ficienter dotatae pro regentium congrua sustentatione, et per Ordinarium in ecclesiastica beneficia confirmatae.''[80]

From the sacred character of oratories as places of divine worship arose their participation in the exemption from civil jurisdiction and in the right of asylum enjoyed by churches. Because the earliest civil[81] and ecclesiastical[82] laws on the right of asylum expressly mention only churches as possessing this right, Van Espen[83] concluded that no other sacred or religious place enjoyed this right in the early Church. But as this right was largely determined and modified by local custom,[84] it is probable that at least in some localities the more important oratories enjoyed it at a very early date. Besides, it is not at all certain that oratories were not included even in these early laws under the terms ''ecclesia'' and ''domus Dei.''[85] This view seems strengthened by a decree of Pope Nicholas II: ''*Sicut antiquitus a sanctis Patribus statutum* est, ita et nos statuimus ut maior ecclesia per circuitum LX passus habeat, *cappellae* vero vel minores ecclesiae XXX. Qui autem confinia eorum infringere tentaverit, aut personam hominis aut bona ejus inde subtraxerit, nisi publicus latro fuerit, quousque emendet, et quod rapuerit reddat, excommunicetur.''[86] Van Espen[87] refers to this decree and admits that the ''cappellae'' are oratories, but questions the authenticity of the decree.[88] At the time of Gratian it is certain that

---

80 Tit. 13, *de consecratione;* Mansi, XXVIII, 338.

81 Very many of these civil laws are cited by Fattolilli, *Theatrum Immunitatis Ecclesiasticae*, p. 507 sq.

82 E. g., Council of Orange (441), c. 5; Mansi, VI, 437; Council of Orleans (541), c. 21; Mansi, XIX, 116; Council of Toledo (681), c. 10; Mansi, XI, 1036.

83 *Dissertatio de Asylo Templorum,* c. 4, § § 1-3; *Scripta Omnia,* IV.

84 Cf. Assemani, *De Ecclesiis,* § 10, art. 8.

85 As used in c. 5, Council of Orange (441); Mansi, VI, 437; c. 10, XII Council of Toledo (681); Mansi, XI, 1036; c. 5, Council of Ravenna (877); Mansi, XVII, 338.

86 C. 6, C. XVII, q. 4; this decree had been promulgated at a Roman Synod held in 1059; Mansi, XIX, 873.

87 *Op. cit.*, c. 3, § § 1-2.

88 His reason for doing so is evident: Pope Nicholas asserts that the ecclesiastical authorities had long since decreed the right of asylum, while Van Espen, a thorough regalist, is endeavoring to show that this right originated with and could be conceded solely by the civil authorities. The authenticity of the decree of Pope Nicholas is not questioned by Mansi nor by the latest edition of Gratian by Richter and Friedberg.

not only churches, but also monasteries, episcopal residences, oratories and cemeteries enjoyed the right of asylum. However, it is just as certain that only those oratories which in reality were and later were also called public oratories enjoyed this right, but not such oratories which were not open to the faithful at large.[89]

Article 5: *Summary of the Status of Oratories Before The Council of Trent.*

Thus far the legislation on oratories has been considered up to the middle of the Sixteenth Century. Before taking up the Tridentine and subsequent legislation, it may be well in a general way to give the status of oratories as they existed prior to the Council of Trent in as far as this can be seen both from the legislation that has been adduced, and also from that which has been investigated but which has not been cited here because of the involved and lengthy form in which it was given. It is only too true that the legislation did not distinguish public from private oratories; still it is certain that some oratories were erected solely for the benefit of an individual or of a family, while others were intended for and were accessible to any of the faithful who chose to use them. Only after the Council of Trent when the distinction between the two classes of oratories assumed great importance did the corresponding distinction in the terms applied to them come into general use.

It is likewise evident that there was little general legislation concerning oratories, most of the laws having been enacted by diocesan, provincial or national councils. As a direct consequence of this, the status of oratories varied greatly not only from century to century, but also from locality to locality. Admitting, therefore, various exceptions at different places and times, the following propositions are advanced as fairly reflecting the general status of oratories before the Council of Trent:

1) Absolute freedom in the erection of oratories was very early abolished, unless the oratory was to serve

---

89 Cf. Schmalzgrueber, *Jus Eccl. Univers.*, L. 3, Tit. 49, n. 109, 131.

solely as a place of prayer; if Mass was to be offered in it, the permission of the bishop was required. 2) After its erection the oratory remained subject to the jurisdiction of the bishop. Hence, his approbation was required for the appointment of the chaplain. 3) The faithful were not free to attend Mass in oratories on Sundays and the principal feasts but were obliged to go to their parish church. 4) On certain special feasts Mass could not be offered in oratories. 5) Oratories that were open to all the faithful enjoyed ecclesiastical immunity. 6) As a rule that admitted very few exceptions no oratory enjoyed the right of a baptismal font. 7) The faithful were not allowed to receive the sacraments of Penance and Holy Communion in an oratory, at least not at Easter time, without the permission of their proper pastor. 8) For the solemnization of Matrimony in an oratory the permission of the bishop was required. 9) Oratories that were succursal chapels were usually free from many of the above limitations. Some enjoyed even the right of a baptismal font without losing their character as chapels of ease. 10) Also the oratories of Religious who by privilege were exempt from the jurisdiction of the bishop were subject to fewer limitations. Thus Religious did not require the permission of the bishop to erect oratories within the confines of their exempt territory. In such oratories they and at least the "familiares" attached to their monastery could at all times fulfil their religious duties regarding the sacraments, the hearing of Mass, etc. The ordinary laity, however, were restricted in the use of even these exempt oratories, though some of the popes removed almost all restrictions from these oratories except in regard to Baptism and the Easter duty. 11) From the Fourth to about the Tenth Century all oratories used for holy Mass were dedicated, but after the Tenth Century only the more important ones. 12) Even oratories that were not dedicated were recognized as possessing a sacred character received through the offering of the holy Sacrifice. As long, therefore, as they were used for this sacred purpose all profane or non-sacred use was to be excluded.

CHAPTER VI.

Legislation on Oratories from the Council of Trent to the Code.

The Council of Trent introduces a new period in the legislation on oratories. This is due not only to its promulgation of a very important law on oratories, but also to the fact that very soon after this Council the various Congregations, Tribunals and Offices of the Roman Curia began to occupy the important position they have ever since held in ecclesiastical affairs. Consequently their enactments, many of which concern oratories, are of supreme importance. It, therefore, no longer will be necessary to consider the legislation of the particular councils which henceforth generally is only a repetition of that of the Tridentine Council and of papal or curial pronouncements. In view of the nature of the Tridentine law, the division of oratories into public and private—which had not been made in the previous legislation—now became a question of great consequence.

Article 1: The Erection of Oratories.

Before the Council of Trent the authorization of the bishop was required and sufficed for the erection of any oratory in which the holy Sacrifice was to be offered. The Council of Trent, however, made a very important change in this matter, for in its decree "Quanta cura" [1] there is the following prohibition: "Neve patiantur episcopi privatis in domibus, atque omnino extra ecclesiam, et ad divinum tantum cultum dedicata oratoria ab eisdem ordinariis designanda et visitanda sanctum sacrificium, a saecularibus aut regularibus quibuscumque peragi." That this decree deprived the bishops of practically all power of authorizing the erection of strictly

[1] Sess. XXII; *"De Observandis et Evitandis in Celebratione Missae."*

private oratories for the celebration of Mass, becomes evident when interpreted in the light of subsequent papal and curial pronouncements of which it will suffice to cite the following:

The Congregation of the Council [2] on March 9, 1577, to the question: "Utrum episcopus, attento conc. Trid. decreto, in oratoriis existentibus in domibus privatorum celebrandi licentiam ex causa concedere possit?" gave the response: "Non posse, sed hanc licentiam petendam esse a Sede Apostolica, praecipue post concilii Trid. communem observantiam." [3] Pope Paul V on October 25, 1615, ordered the following declaration of the same Congregation to be sent to all bishops: "Tametsi S. C. C., optimis innixa rationibus, saepissime responderit, celebrandi licentias in privatis oratoriis non nisi a Sede Apostolica esse concedendas . . . Illmi Patres, SSmi D. N. jussu, significandum duxerunt, facultatem hujusmodi licentias dandi, ipsius concilii decreto unicuique ademptam esse, solique beatissimo Romano Pontifici esse reservatam." [3] The Congregation of the Council reiterated this declaration when it stated on May 27, 1617: "Non posse episcopum ex quavis causa cuique concedere ut sacrum fiat in privatis oratoriis." [4] Finally, the Congregation of Rites on September 20, 1749, gave a negative response to the question: "An episcopi, non habentes facultatem specialem concedendi licentiam celebrandi Missam in oratoriis privatis et cappellis pro saecularibus et aliis, possint licentiam petentibus concedere?" [5]

In view of the above and similar pronouncements of the Holy See, it appeared that a bishop (unless he possessed special delegated faculties) under no circumstances could allow Mass in private oratories. However, canon-

---

2 The substance of the decisions of this Congregation that will be cited in this chapter can be found in Pallottini (*Collectio Conclusionum et Resolutionum* S. C. C., XIV, s. v. "Oratorium") as well as in the authors that will be referred to for each decision.

3 Cf. Many, *De Locis Sacris*, n. 80; Gattico, *De Oratoriis Dom.*, c. 14, n. 6.

4 Cf. Gasparri, *De SS. Eucharistia*, I, n. 225.

5 § 5; D. A., 2404.

ists[6] were almost unanimous in maintaining that for a grave reason and "per modum actus" the bishop could grant this privilege. This common opinion was confirmed by a decision of the Congregation of the Council on December 20, 1856.[7] Prior to this decision there were a number of particular decisions of the Congregation of the Propaganda[8] allowing missionaries to offer the holy Sacrifice in private houses if they had a sufficiently grave reason and obtained the permission of their Vicar or Prefect Apostolic. Apart from these exceptional cases, the bishops no longer enjoyed the power of permitting the celebration of Mass in private oratories. But precisely which oratories were considered private and which were considered public? At least a partial answer to this henceforth important question can be derived from a closer investigation of the Tridentine decree and of the subsequent decisions of the Roman Curia.

The Council of Trent legislated against bishops allowing Mass to be celebrated "Privatis in domibus, atque omnino extra ecclesiam, et ad divinum tantum cultum dedicata oratoria ab eisdem ordinariis designanda et visitanda."[9] Hence papal permission was required to offer Mass: 1) In private houses, whether in or outside an oratory erected therein. 2) In non-private houses if the place in question was neither a church nor an oratory dedicated to divine worship. Thus far the law seems clear, though some authors[10] united the two prohibitions and interpreted the words of the Council of Trent to mean that bishops could not allow Mass "Privatis in domibus extra ecclesiam et oratoria," thus implying that they could allow it in an oratory in a private house. But this view was patently contrary to the re-

---

6 Cf. Barbosa, *De Officio Episcopi*, Alleg. XXIII, n. 7-9; Suarez, *De Eucharistia*, Disp. LXXXI, Sect. III, § 3; Schmalzgrueber, *Jus Eccl. Univers.*, L. 3, Tit. 40, n. 8-12; St. Alphonse, *Theol. Moral.*, L. 6, n. 359; Gattico, *De Oratoriis Dom.*, c. 15.

7 Cf. Many, *De Locis Sacris*, n. 81.

8 Dec. 14, 1668, April 30, 1753, Sept. 6, 1821, and June 3, 1828; Collectanea, 172, 388, 764 and 805.

9 Sess. XXII, decr. "*Quanta cura.*"

10 Zypaeus, Vasquez, Lessius, Amicus and others cited by Pasqualigo, *De Sacrificio*, I, Quaest. 447, n. 1.

sponse quoted above from the Congregation of the Council of March 9, 1577.

Hence of the threefold power which bishops enjoyed before the Council of Trent of allowing Mass: 1) In oratories of private houses: 2) In oratories of non-private houses: 3) Elsewhere within non-private houses—the first and third now were reserved to the Holy See and bishops retained only the power of allowing Mass in oratories of non-private houses. How extensive was this power? In order to answer this question, it is necessary to investigate what was meant by the "domus privata" of the Tridentine decree. These words signified the dwelling of an individual or of a private family in distinction to a "domus communis, seu publica, seu non privata" which usually designated the dwelling of a community or a building that was open to the public.[11] But as many doubts arose, Rome was required to answer a number of questions more clearly defining "domus privata" and "domus non privata," the more important of which were determined as follows:

1) Episcopal residences were not private houses in the sense in which the Council of Trent used this term, "Cum haec sub privatarum domorum nomine nunquam censeri possint."[12] Hence no papal permission was required for the erection of oratories in such residences as was expressly declared by the Congregation of the Council in 1623.[13]

2) The same Congregation repeatedly declared that the palaces of civil magistrates, nobles, princes, etc., were private houses and that consequently the permission of the Holy See was required to erect oratories therein.[14] But if the oratories in such private houses were erected as ecclesiastical benefices and were conferred in title, they were not private, but public oratories,[15] otherwise,

11 Cf. Gasparri, *De SS. Eucharistia,* I, n. 212.

12 Benedict XIV, ep. encycl. "*Magno cum,*" June 2, 1751, § 2; Fontes, 413.

13 Cf. Benedict XIV, *De SS. Missae Sacrificio,* L. 3, c. 6, n. 2.

14 Cf. the decisions of Feb. 12, 1577, July 6, 1615, Feb. 12, 1616, Nov. 14, 1658, as quoted by Gattico, *De Oratoriis Dom.,* c. 16, n. 2-7.

15 Cf. the decisions of S. C. C., Jan. 15, 1616, June 15, 1616, and July 28, 1619, as quoted by Pignatelli, *Consultationes Canonicae,* I, Consult, 93, n. 24.

a benefice could not be erected therein. As public oratories they had to be made accessible to the faithful and, therefore, had to possess a public entrance.[16]

3) Seminaries and houses of Spiritual Retreat erected by the authority of the bishop, hospitals, orphanages and similar "loca pia" even though erected only upon laic authority and also public prisons were not to be considered as private houses, neither was the permission of the Holy See required for the erection of their oratories.[17]

4) Monasteries of Religious Orders as Religious houses never were considered as private houses in the meaning of the Council of Trent; hence papal permission patently was unnecessary for celebrating Mass in their oratories. The same principle was extended to all Religious Congregations in virtue of several decisions [18] regarding particular Congregations, and finally also to Communities living in common without vows.[19] The exact status of the granges ("granciae") or rural houses of the Religious was somewhat more complicated, as they scarcely could be called Religious houses in view of the fact that they were not canonically erected as such. Abstracting from privileges to the contrary obtained after the Council of Trent, these granges as a rule were considered as private houses and, therefore, a papal indult was required for the erection of their oratories.[20]

But despite the above and many other decisions, new doubts constantly were arising. These were due to the fact that the division of oratories into only two classes, private and public, was not an adequate one. For many

---

16 Cf. De Bonis, *De Oratoriis Pub.*, n. 331-338.

17 S. C. C., July 11, 1620, for Seminaries; S. C. C., April 5, 1851, for houses of Retreat; S. C. Reg., Feb. 18, 1628, for hospitals; S. C. C., March 27,1847, for orphanages and smilar "loca pia"; S. C. C., Nov. 14, 1618, for prisons; cf. Gattico, *De Oratcriis Dom.*, c. 16, and Gasparri, *De SS. Eucharistia,* I, n. 213.

18 S. C. C., Aug. 15, 1615, and Aug. 7, 1649; cf. Gattico, *De Oratoriis Dom.*, c. 16, n. 15.

19 Cf. Gasparri, *De SS. Eucharistia,* I, n. 213.

20 For a more extensive discussion of these granges, cf. Fagnani, *Commentaria in Libros Decretalium* (c. 27, X, *de censibus*, III, 39), *Disceptatio de Grangiis et earum Oratoriis;* Pasqualigo, *De Sacrificio*, 1, Quaest. 488-491.

of the oratories that Rome declared were not private in the sense that papal permission was not required for their erection, nevertheless, were not recognized as public in the sense that they were to be accessible to all the faithful with the accompanying rights that this implied. Hence canonists began to call such oratories non-private, semi-private or semi-public oratories. These terms Rome also used occasionally, but it was not until the decree of the Congregation of Rites of January 23, 1899,[21] that the term semi-public oratory was officially adopted and defined. As the definitions given in this decree apparently constitute the principal source for those contained in canon 1188 of the Code, this decree will be considered later in connection with that canon. Meanwhile, in virtue of all that has been stated, at least a general idea can be formed of the nature of a private and of a non-private oratory.[22]

The decree "Quanta cura" not only greatly influenced private oratories by demanding papal permission for their erection, but it also had definite effects on the status of non-private oratories in as far as it declared that they were to be dedicated to divine worship and were to be designated and visited by the bishop. For secular oratories these conditions were but slightly different from what they had been, but they were quite new and severe for the oratories of Religious. For in virtue not of the existing law but rather of contrary privileges,[23] Religious had been universally recognized as possessing the right of erecting oratories for celebrating Mass anywhere in their monasteries without being subject to any limitation or visitation by the bishop. And yet, that Religious were now subject to the conditions exacted by the Council

---

21 D. A., 4007.

22 As is indicated, the term non-private oratory is used here to include all oratories for whose erection papal permission was not required.

23 Obtained by direct papal concession or through the so-called communication of privileges.

of Trent could not be questioned as they were mentioned expressly in the Tridentine decree. Moreover, the decree itself indicated that even long existing privileges did not excuse from its observance, for the bishops were empowered by the Council itself as delegates of the Holy See to provide that this decree was faithfully observed "Non obstantibus privilegiis, exemptionibus, appellationibus, ac consuetudinibus quibuscumque." [24] Hence all non-private oratories were now subject to the same law. But in the course of time, at least the Religious Orders again obtained new privileges from various popes [25] who granted them the right of erecting oratories in their houses independently of the bishop whose rights of designation and visitation were transferred to their own Religious Superiors. But the law only is under consideration here, not these particular privileges contrary to the law.

By the Tridentine law, therefore, these non-private oratories had to be designated by the bishop. In this they now differed from private oratories granted by a papal indult which permitted the grantee to erect the oratory in any part of the house that he preferred, provided it was approved by the bishop when he inspected it before the holy Sacrifice was offered there. Moreover, they were subject to the regular canonical visitation of the bishop, in which they again differed from private oratories.[26] Finally, they were to be dedicated to divine worship alone. This implied both the exclusion of all domestic use and at least some stability and permanence in their use as places of divine worship.

Article 2: Limitations and Rights of Oratories.

Having investigated the legislation on the erection of oratories in the previous article, their rights and limitations must yet be considered. As the two classes of oratories enjoyed different rights and were subjected to dif-

---

24 Sess. XXII, decr. "*Quanta cura.*"

25 The earliest grant was that of Gregory XIII, const. "*Decet Romanum Pontificem,*" May 3, 1575, to the Jesuits; cf. Pasqualigo, *De Sacrificio*, I, Quaest. 484, who cites about twenty authors to prove that all Regulars participated in this grant.

26 Cf. Gattico, *De Oratoriis Dom.*, c. 24, n. 11.

ferent limitations, they must now be treated separately; but as it will be necessary to refer to much of this matter when examining the legislation in the Code, it will be given here only in a very succinct and summary manner.

Section 1: Of Private Oratories.

The Apostolic indult granting the privilege of a private oratory always contained certain limitations which were expressed explicitly or in general terms; in the latter case they were to be interpreted according to the norms laid down by the Holy See.[27] The most important of these limitations together with the few rights enjoyed by private oratories were the following:

1) Before Mass could be offered in a private oratory it had to be visited by the bishop or his delegate "inspiciendi gratia, num decens, et apte compositum sit, et num aliquid eorum, quae necessaria sunt, in eodem desit." [28] Unless the indult provided otherwise, only one Mass could be offered daily;[29] this was to be a Low Mass ("Missa lecta") and had to be offered in the presence of at least one of the principally privileged persons,[30] i. e., of those persons to whom the privilege of the private oratory was conceded and who were named in the indult. In only one contingency (unless the indult expressly granted other exceptions) could Mass be offered in their absence, namely, if otherwise it would be very difficult to obtain Holy Viaticum for the dying.[31] On the more solemn feasts Mass could not be offered in these oratories.[32]

---

27 Especially those contained in the decrees "*Quoniam sancta sancte tractanda sunt,*" Dec. 15, 1703, of Clement XI (Bened. XIV Bull., IX, 29) and "*Cum duo nobiles,*" Jan. 7, 1741, of Benedict XIV (Bened. XIV Bull., XIII, Suppl., 220); in the ep. encycl. "*Magno cum,*" June 2, 1751, of Benedict XIV (Fontes, 413) and in various decisions of the Roman Curia.

28 Benedict XIV, ep. encycl. "*Magno cum,*" § 12; cf. note 27.

29 Clement XI, decr. "*Quoniam sancta sancte tractanda sunt*"; cf. note 27.

30 Benedict XIV, decr. "*Cum duo nobiles*"; cf. note 27.

31 S. R. C., Aug. 27, 1836, § 7; D. A., 2745.

32 Clement XI, decr. "*Quoniam sancta sancte tractanda sunt*"; cf. note 27; S. R. C., Feb. 13, 1892, and April 10, 1896; D. A., 3767 and 3896.

2) The obligation of hearing Mass could be fulfilled in a private oratory only by the privileged persons and by those whose presence was necessary for the service of the celebrant or for the convenience of the privileged persons.[33] Usually the indult granted this right not only to the principally privileged persons as defined above, but also to the simply privileged persons, i. e., to their relatives (by consanguinity or affinity to the fourth degree inclusive) who lived with the principally privileged persons as members of the family. It also as a rule was extended to the noble guests of the principally privileged persons.[34]

3) Holy Communion could be administered in private oratories only if the papal indult expressly granted this right or if the bishop permitted it. However, a few years prior to the Code, general permission to this effect was given by the Pope of Frequent Communion, Pius X.[35] If the papal indult granted also the right of reserving the Blessed Sacrament, it was necessary that Mass be offered daily in the oratory; if this was impossible, a further indult had to be obtained from the Holy See which then usually demanded that Mass be offered there at least once a week.[36]

4) The sacraments of Baptism and Penance[37] could be administered in these oratories only in virtue of a special permission of the bishop or in the presence of such circumstances as would warrant their administration in any private house.

5) Matrimony could be celebrated in private oratories only with the permission of the bishop and "Si nullum immineat periculum ac laudabiles concurrant causae."[38] Under these conditions also the nuptial Mass could be celebrated.[39]

---

33 Benedict XIV, decr. "*Cum duo nobiles*"; cf. note 27.

34 Cf. Gattico, *De Oratoriis Dom.*, c. 25; Many, *De Locis Sacris*, n. 90; *Eph. Liturg.*, XXIV (1910), 133.

35 S. R. C., May 8, 1907; D. A., 4201.

36 S. R. C., May 14, 1889; D. A., 3706.

37 Benedict XIV, ep. encycl. "*Magno cum*," §§ 19-20; cf. note 27.

38 S. R. C., Aug. 31, 1872, § 2; D. A., 3265.

39 *Ibid.*, § 3.

6) Other functions, such as sermons, the distribution of palms, candles and ashes, the "Benedictio mulieris post partum," the aspersion with holy water, the functions of Holy Week, the exposition of the Blessed Sacrament, etc., were not allowed except with special permission.[40]

7) These oratories were not to be used for domestic purposes;[41] nevertheless they did not enjoy ecclesiastical immunity.[42]

8) Finally, they were to be neither consecrated nor solemnly blessed.[43]

Section 2: Of Non-private Oratories.

In general, the rights of non-private oratories were more extensive, and their limitations less restrictive than those of private oratories as enumerated above. These rights and limitations may be summarized as follows:

1) Strictly public oratories, i. e., such as were to be accessible to all the faithful, had to possess an entrance from some public thoroughfare, or if the oratory could not be entered except through a courtyard or atrium, then at least this courtyard or atrium had to be public.[44]

2) Such strictly public oratories had to be consecrated or solemnly blessed.[45] There was no necessity, however, of consecrating or solemnly blessing other non-private oratories,[46] in fact, both seem to have been forbidden until the end of the last century.[47]

40 Cf. Gattico, *De Oratoriis Dom.*, c. 28, and the decisions and decrees he there alleges.

41 "In oratorio ab omnibus domesticis usibus libero"; this or a similar clause has been found in all papal indults of a private oratory.

42 C. Ep. et Reg., Nov. 7, 1617; cf. Barbosa, *Jus Eccl. Univers.*, L. 2, c. 3, n. 68; Pignatelli, *Consultationes Canonicae*, I, Consult. 93, n. 2.

43 S. R. C., June 5, 1899, § 6; D. A., 4025.

44 S. C. C., Nov. 13, 1626, Aug. 3, 1685, June 28, 1724 and Feb. 12, 1735; cf. Many, *De Locis Sacris*, n. 66.

45 S. R. C., June 5, 1899, § 2; D. A., 4025.

46 Nor were they subject to the above prescription concerning a public entrance.

47 S. R. C., March 11, 1820, § 10 (Gardellini, n. 4565); July 27, 1888 (Collectanea [ed. 1893] 1591); Nov. 29, 1878 and June 5, 1899, § 5 (D. A., 3471 and 4025).

3) When erecting these oratories the bishop could place limitations concerning the time, kind and number of daily Masses that could be offered there;[48] but after their erection, as a rule he was not to impose any restrictions.[49] However, the pastor in whose parish the oratory was situated had no power in this matter unless the oratory was subject to him "speciali jure" or was erected within his parish church.[50]

4) That the faithful could fulfil their obligation by attending Mass in any of these oratories on Sundays and even the most solemn feast days was admitted not only in virtue of general custom, but was also in the course of time expressly stated by the Holy See.[51] Nevertheless, the Council of Trent declared that the faithful were to be admonished to do so in their own parish church.[52]

5) Ecclesiastical functions that were strictly parochial were forbidden; all other non-parochial or merely sacerdotal functions could be performed in any non-private oratory independently of the pastor in whose territory the oratory was situated, unless it was erected in the parish church itself. This was declared in a general decree of the Congregation of Rites, January 12, 1704.[53] The blessing of the baptismal font, solemn Mass on Maundy Thursday, conducting processions through the parish (and the blessing of homes on Holy Saturday) were enumerated among the parochial functions.[54] Non-

48 S. R. C., June 14, 1845; D. A., 2893.

49 S. C. C., Aug. 3, 1675, and Sept. 8, 1724; cf. Gasparri, *De SS. Eucharistia*, I, n. 126, 192, 197, 204.

50 S. R. C., Nov. 20, 1628, and April 21, 1635; D. A., 484 and 619.

51 In oratories erected in the episcopal palace, even "absente episcopo vel sede vacante," by S. R. C., July 2, 1661; D. A., 1196; in any oratory of any bishop, residential or titular, by S. R. C., June 8, 1896; D. A., 3906; in oratories of Religious, by S. C. Ep. et Reg., May 31, 1602, and May 25, 1618, and by S. C. C., Aug. 8, 1615 and March 6, 1621; cf. Ferraris, *Bibliotheca*, V, s. v. "Missa," § 16, n. 12; in oratories of Sodalities, by S. R. C., May 22, 1841; D. A., 2832; finally in any non-private oratory, by the general decree of the S. R. C., Jan. 23, 1899; D. A., 4007.

52 Sess. XXII, decr. "*Quanta cura.*"

53 § § 2-4; D. A., 2123. This decree directly and immediately referred to oratories of Confraternities, but its regulations were applicable also to other non-private oratories as was stated by the same Congregation, March 3, 1866; Gardellini, n. 5361.

54 S. R. C., Jan. 12, 1704, § § 6, 8, 22, and March 15, 1721; D. A., 2123 and 2270.

parochial functions, and, therefore, permissible in these oratories, were the exposition of the Blessed Sacrament for the Forty Hours' Devotion, sermons, the blessing and distribution of candles, palms and ashes, and the "Benedictio mulieris post partum." [55]

6) The Blessed Sacrament could not be reserved even in strictly public oratories unless this privilege was obtained from the Holy See or from the local Ordinary if by papal indult he had obtained the faculty of granting this privilege.[56]

7) Even strictly public oratories did not obtain any more extensive rights concerning the administration of Baptism and the celebration of Matrimony than private oratories.

8) In all non-private oratories confessors approved by the bishop could administer the sacrament of Penance; Holy Communion, likewise, could be distributed there.[57] However, the ancient restriction limiting the preceptive Paschal Communion to one's proper parish (or at least demanding the permission of the bishop or pastor if It was to be received elsewhere) was retained.[58]

9) Finally, these oratories enjoyed ecclesiastical immunity and especially the right of asylum.[59]

---

55 S. R. C., Jan. 12, 1704, §§ 5, 6, 11, 18, and Nov. 21, 1893; D. A., 2123 and 3813.

56 S. R. C., Sept. 12, 1626, and March 8, 1879; D. A., 420 and 3484.

57 S. R. C., Nov. 22, 1710, § 7, March 10, 1714, § 7, and July 9, 1718, § 1; D. A., 2208, 2224 and 2251.

58 Clement X, const. "*Superna,*" June 21, 1670, §§ 4-7; Benedict XIV, ep. encycl. "*Magno cum,*" June 2, 1751, §§ 20-24; Pius X, const. "*Tradita ab antiquis,*" Sept. 14, 1912, § 4; Fontes, 246, 413 and 698.

59 Gregory XIV, const. "*Cum alias,*" May 24, 1591; Benedict XIV, const. "*Officii nostri,*" March 15, 1750; Fontes, 172 and 406. Cf. Barbosa, *Jus Eccl. Univers.*, L. 2, c. 3, n. 67 sq.; Farinacius, *De Immunitate Ecclesiarum*, c. 17; Schmalzgrueber, *Jus Eccl. Univers.*, L. 3, Tit. 49, n. 109 sq.

PART III.

The Code Legislation on Oratories.

Praenotanda.

For the first time in the history of ecclesiastical legislation oratories are given a separate and avowedly explicit treatise in the Code. This is found in Book III, Title X, Canons 1188-1196. The advantages of this are obvious. Prior to the Code oratories were indeed frequently the subject of legislation, but they were almost invariably treated incidentally, that is, laws were enacted concerning them because of their relation to some other subject that was primarily under consideration. This necessarily precluded a unified and comprehensive legislation on oratories; it concomitantly effected that the laws that were enacted were more or less unrelated, being scattered throughout the field of canonical subjects.

The Code in offering its legislation on oratories under a separate title to a large extent has obviated the difficulties and deficiencies resulting from the older method of presenting the legislation pertinent to oratories. There are some canons of the Code referring to oratories that are found outside of the title that legislates on them exclusively; these canons, however, either are referred to in the tract on oratories or they are of comparatively minor importance in their relation to oratories.

The legislation of the Code on oratories is by no means new in its entirety; on the contrary, most of its prescriptions are but a restatement of the pre-Code law given in clearer terms and more concise form. The Code as a whole, though it does contain many new laws, is not and was not intended to be a body of entirely new laws; it is rather a collection and modification of already existing laws as it itself clearly states in canon 6, § 1.

If this is true of the Code as a whole, it is especially true of its laws on oratories. The Code made a few changes in the pre-existing laws, but none of these changes are as important or as extensive as those introduced by the decree "Quanta cura" of the Council of Trent.[1] The importance of the Code legislation on oratories is to be found not in its departure from the old law, but in its codification of the immense body of laws on oratories in a few concise and succinct canons.

In canon 6, § § 2-4 the Code itself not only warrants but also demands that its laws be interpreted in the light of the old laws in as far as the latter are in harmony with and form the basis of the former. Hence in view of the fact that the pre-Code legislation has been investigated at some length in the preceding pages, an interpretation of the Code law which does not radically differ from it will now be rendered less difficult.

The legislation of the Code will be investigated here in four chapters under the captions: 1) Definitions and kinds of oratories. 2) The laws governing public oratories. 3) The laws governing semi-public oratories. 4) The laws governing private oratories.

---

1 Cf. above, Chapter VI.

CHAPTER VII.

Definitions and Kinds of Oratories.

The Holy See, cognizant of the unsatisfactory definitions that had been offered by canonists in previous centuries,[1] fully realized the importance of accurately distinguishing and authoritatively defining the various classes of oratories before presenting their specific legislation. Hence canon 1188, the introductory canon of the Code to its brief treatise on oratories, contains a definition of an oratory, the division of oratories into public, semi-public and private, and a definition of each.

Article 1: Definition and Nature of an Oratory.

Oratorium est locus divino cultui destinatus, non tamen eo potissimum fine ut universo fidelium populo usui sit ad religionem publice colendam (can. 1188, § 1).

This definition is certainly an improvement over the traditional definition of an oratory as a "locus aptus ad orandum"[2] which was too general and comprehensive to be satisfactory. The Code's definition is general enough to include the three kinds of oratories and at the same time is sufficiently specific to differentiate it from all other places, whether sacred or profane. Analysing the Code's definition more closely it is found to comprise two parts:

1) *Oratorium est locus divino cultui destinatus*: This is the genus of the definition, or as Vermeersch-Creusen[3] call it, the positive element, which differentiates an oratory from a profane place. Nevertheless the Code carefully abstains from calling an oratory a sacred place,

---

[1] Cf. above, Chapters III and IV.
[2] Cf. above, Chapter III.
[3] *Epitome,* II, n. 497.

and it does so despite the fact that this definition as well as the entire tract on oratories is given under the general caption "De Locis Sacris."[4] The reason for this is obvious. Canon 1154 states: "Loca sacra ea sunt quae divino cultui (fideliumve sepulturae) deputantur consecratione vel benedictione quam probati liturgici libri ad hoc praescribunt." But semi-public oratories need not and private oratories cannot be consecrated or blessed.[5] Hence there are some oratories which are not "loca sacra" in the canonical acceptation of the term. Probably for the same reason the Code uses the verb "destinatus" in its definition of an oratory in preference to "dedicatus" which it uses in canon 1161 in defining a church.[6] Churches and oratories have this in common that they are at least destined (if not also dedicated) to divine worship; of no other place, sacred or profane, can this be predicated. Hence the first part of the Code's definition of an oratory adequately differentiates it from all other places except churches; this further differentiation is made in the second part of the definition.

2) *Non tamen eo potissimum fine ut universo fidelium populo usui sit ad religionem publice colendam*: This constitutes what is really the principal difference between an oratory and a church. A glance at the Code's definition of a church will suffice to render this more evident. "Ecclesiae nomine intelligitur aedes sacra divino cultui dedicata eum potissimum in finem ut omnibus Christifidelibus usui sit ad divinum cultum publice exercendum" (can. 1161). The definition of a church and of an oratory are formulated in such a manner as to offer a direct contrast to each other. A church is intended "pro omnibus Christifidelibus;" an oratory is intended primarily only for certain determined persons, that is, "non pro universo fidelium populo." For even in the case of a public oratory where the right of all the faithful is recognized by law, the oratory is intended primarily for cer-

4 This being the title in the Code of Section I, Part II, Book III, in which the tract on oratories is given.

5 Except with the ordinary blessing of houses; cf. can. 1196.

6 Cf. Barin, *Commentarium, Eph. Liturg.*, XXXIX (1925), 368.

tain determined persons and only secondarily for all the faithful. This is sufficiently evident from the canons themselves and is emphasized by nearly every author who comments on them.

Among the authors who emphasize this essential element of difference are Ferreres: "Differt ecclesia ab oratorio quod illa primario aedificata est communi fidelium utilitati (et hoc constituit differentiam formalem), oratorium vero utilitati alicuius communitatis, aut generis personarum."[7] A Coronata: "Differentia in hoc proprie est quod oratorium principaliter pro determinatis personis erectum est."[8] Vermeersch-Creusen: "Ecclesiae propter publicum cultum a Christifidelibus exercendum dedicatae sunt; prima intentione conduntur propter fideles, dum oratoria vel non omnes Christifideles admittunt, vel, quamvis omnes admittant, diversa tamen intentione sunt erecta: e. g. ad honorandam imaginem sanctam, propter confraternitatis commoditatem."[9] Raus: "Prima intentione non propter peculiarem alium finem cōnduntur ecclesiae nisi ratione publici cultus ab omnibus fidelibus exercendi; et in hoc discernuntur ab oratoriis et cappellis."[10] Cocchi: "Oratorium ab ecclesia discrepat in eo quod erectio oratorii saltem prima intentione non fiat ad universi populi usum."[11] Bouuaert-Simenon: "Distinctio inter ecclesias et oratoria in eo consistit quod primae universo populo destinatur, et altera tantum communitati seu privatis personis."[12]

The reason the Code and its commentators so emphatically stress this element is the fact that for centuries it was not recognized as constituting the formal and essential difference between a church and an oratory. Formerly canonists either offered no means of differentiation, or they endeavored to distinguish churches from oratories by what were in reality only accidental and by

---

7 *Institutiones,* II, n. 94.
8 *De Locis et Temp. Sacris,* n. 69.
9 *Epitome,* II, n. 475.
10 *Institutiones,* n. 217.
11 *Commentarium,* V, n. 28.
12 *Manuale,* n. 787.

no means necessary and universal differences. Thus they pointed out that churches were consecrated and endowed, while oratories were neither consecrated nor endowed; that churches were erected principally for the celebration of holy Mass, while oratories were intended primarily as places of prayer. Pirhing, Tuschus, Verani and Fagnani were cited on this question in Chapter III, where some of the defects of their differentiations were indicated. For, as was shown, even at the time of these authors many oratories were both consecrated and endowed, while at least some churches lacked either consecration, endowment, or both. Moreover, it is likewise certain that at their time some oratories were erected primarily and were used almost exclusively as places for the celebration of holy Mass rather than as places of prayer, prescinding, of course, from the fact that the holy Sacrifice is the greatest of prayers. Thus the *raison d'être* of an entire class of oratories, the so-called chantry chapels, was the celebration of Requiem Masses for a certain deceased person. Hence the means of differentiation which the authors formerly offered failed to differentiate, at least in some instances.

The means of differentiation, however, which the Code gives is absolute and universal: if the place destined for divine worship is intended primarily for all the faithful it is a church; if not, it is an oratory.[13] This principle of distinction is of comparatively recent date, having been clearly formulated for the first time in a particular decision of the Congregation of Rites, July 22, 1855, which declared: "Ecclesia intelligitur, quae eo potissimum fine aedificatur, ut publico fidelis populi usui deserviat. Cappella publica vero, quae licet ingressum habeat in publica via, attamen non tam fidelis populi libero usui destinata videtur, quam alicuius Familiae, vel Collegii commoditati."[14] The distinction was made here

13 In applying this principle, cases may possibly arise in which it may be difficult to determine for whom the place of worship was primarily intended. But such doubts are "dubia facti" not "dubia juris" and are possible in the application of any law.

14 Gardellini, n. 5215, § 3.

between public oratories and churches, but held "a fortiori" for other oratories.

Besides this essential difference between a church and an oratory, the Code seems to indicate two other differences when in its definitions it calls a church an "aedes sacra" and an oratory a "locus." Reference already has been made to the omission of the word "sacer" in the Code's definition of an oratory; while the fact that a church is called an edifice and an oratory is called a place indicates at most only a very accidental difference and one which by no means is always present. Hence the assertion of Barin cannot be urged too strongly when he writes: "Ecclesia dicitur *aedes,* distincte enim debet esse ab aliis aedificiis et per se materialiter formare aedificium, dum oratorium non necessario distinctum et separatum ad aliis aedibus esse debet, quinimo dantur oratoria quae intra domesticos parietes, in angulis domus privatae erecta sunt, et minimam partem aedificii profani occupant: proinde oratorium non dicitur *aedes* sed *locus.*"[15] For not only are many oratories separate and distinct buildings, but there are also churches which occupy only a minor part of the building in which they are located; this is verified especially in the case of the so-called combination church and school buildings so prevalent in mission and quasi-mission territory. Hence the principal and only certain difference between an oratory and a church consists in this that the former is not intended—at least not primarily—for the public worship of all the faithful.

---

[15] *Commentarium, Eph. Liturg.,* XXXIX (1925), 368.

Article 2: Kinds of Oratories; Their Definition and Nature.

Est vero oratorium:

1° PUBLICUM, si praecipue erectum sit in commodum alicuius collegii aut etiam privatorum, ita tamen ut omnibus fidelibus, tempore saltem divinorum officiorum, ius sit, legitime comprobatum, illud adeundi;

2° SEMI-PUBLICUM, si in commodum alicuius communitatis vel coetus fidelium eo convenientium erectum sit, neque liberum cuique sit illud adire;

3° PRIVATUM seu DOMESTICUM, si in privatis aedibus in commodum alicuius tantum familiae vel personae privatae erectum sit (can. 1188, § 2).

This threefold division of oratories will not be found in the works of any of the older canonists as they divided oratories into only two classes, public and private.[16] The term semi-public oratory was used officially for the first time in a particular decree of the Congregation of Rites, March 8, 1879;[17] but the triple division of oratories was "canonized" only on January 23, 1899, when the same Congregation issued the following general decree:[18]

Constat oratoria publica ea esse, quae auctoritate Ordinarii ad publicum Dei cultum perpetuo dedicata, benedicta vel etiam solemniter consecrata, ianuam habent in via, vel liberum a publica via fidelibus universim pandunt ingressum. Privata e contra stricto sensu dicuntur oratoria, quae in privatis aedibus in commodum alicuius personae vel familiae ex indulto Sanctae Sedis erecta sunt. Quae medium inter haec duo locum tenent, ut nomen ipsum indicata, oratoria semi-publica sunt et vocantur.

Ut autem quaelibet ambiguitas circa haec oratoria amoveatur, S. D. N. Leo Papa XIII ex Sacrorum Rituum Congregationis consulto, statuit et declaravit: Oratoria semi-publica ea esse, quae etsi in loco quodammodo privato, vel non absolute publico, auctoritate Ordinarii erecta sunt; commodo tamen non omnium fidelium nec privatae tantum personae aut familiae, sed alicuius communitatis vel personarum coetus inserviunt . . . . Huius

16 Cf. above, Chapter IV.

17 § 7, n. 3; D. A., 3484.

18 D. A., 4007.

generis oratoria sunt quae pertinent ad Seminaria et Collegia ecclesiastica; ad pia Instituta et Societates votorum simplicium, aliasque Communitates sub regula sive statutis saltem ab Ordinario approbatis; ad Domus spiritualibus exercitiis addictis; ad Convictus et Hospitia juventuti litteris, scientiis aut artibus instituendae destinata; ad Nosocomia, Orphanotrophia, nec non ad Arces et Carceres; atque similia oratoria, in quibus ex instituto aliquis Christifidelium coetus convenire solet ad audiendam Missam. Quibus adjungi debent cappellae, in coemeterio rite erectae, dummodo in Missae celebratione non iis tantum ad quos pertinet, sed aliis etiam fidelibus aditus pateat.

This decree constitutes the principal and immediate source for the Code's threefold division of oratories; it likewise affords the essential elements for the definitions of the Code, though the Code departs from it in a few particulars.[19] As public, semi-public and private oratories have their own proper legislation, their definitions as given by the Code are of sufficient importance to warrant a close examination.

A **public oratory**, therefore, is an oratory erected principally for the convenience of a certain corporation, or even of private individuals, but in such a manner that all the faithful have the right—when legitimately established [20]—to frequent it, at least at the time of divine services. In this definition the Code again clearly indicates the essential factor which differentiates a public (or any other) oratory from a church. A public oratory may be erected for the convenience of private persons or for the benefit of a corporation or moral person. In view of this,

---

19 E. g., by not demanding that a public oratory have an entrance from a public thoroughfare, by classifying the oratories in cemeteries referred to in can. 1190 as private, etc.

20 The perfect participle "comprobatum" of can. 1188, § 2, 1°, is used predicatively and as such must be interpreted here as representing a subordinate clause, either conditional or temporal. It is thus interpreted by Augustine (*Commentary*, VI, 66), A Coronata (*De Locis et Temp. Sacris*, n. 72), Vermeersch-Creusen (*Epitome*, II, n. 498), Blat (*Commentarium*, IV, n. 40), Cocchi (*Commentarium*, V, n. 29), Barin (*Commentarium*, *Eph. Liturg.*, XXXIX [1925], 372) and other commentators on the Code. In fact, Woywod seems to be the only author who considers it used attributively, as he evidently does when he translates the passage in question by: "All the faithful have a legitimately established right (*Commentary*, II, n. 1225)." His rendition in a previous work (*The New Canon Law*, n. 1031) is equally inaccurate.

A Coronata[21] and Bouuaert-Simenon[22] assert that there are consequently two species of public oratories. Such a sub-distinction, however, is not only very accidental, but also is of no practical importance as all public oratories are governed by the same laws. Moreover, it can reasonably be disputed whether the legislator intended to make this sub-distinction. Most public oratories have been and still are erected for the primary benefit of a corporation, and consequently, unless the Code mentioned that they could be erected also for the primary benefit of private individuals, this possibility might have been doubted, especially in view of the fact that the Code declares an oratory to be private "Si in privatis aedibus in commodum alicuius tantum familiae vel personae privatae erectum sit" (can. 1188, § 2, 3°). Hence the Code may be intending to forestall this doubt rather than to formulate a new sub-distinction, though it must be conceded that the mere wording of the definition warrants the assertion and sub-distinction made by A Coronata and Bouuaert-Simenon.

Though a public oratory is not erected primarily for the benefit of all the faithful, nevertheless they have the right to frequent it at least at the time of divine services. It is in this right of the faithful that a public oratory is distinguished from a semi-public oratory, for the fact that they are subject to different laws is consequent to rather than constitutive of their essential difference. If an oratory is open to the faithful by the merely gratuitous indulgence of its proprietor it is not a public oratory; for in order to be public the faithful must have a strict right to frequent it and its proprietor must be bound by the corresponding obligation of not interfering with the free exercise of this right, and consequently, of affording an unimpeded admission to the faithful. Both the right and the correlative obligation are perpetual.[23] However,

---

21 *De Locis et Temp. Sacris,* n. 72.

22 *Manuale,* n. 787.

23 Cf. Many, *De Locis Sacris,* n. 73; Barin, *Commentarium, Eph. Liturg.,* XXXIX (1925), 372.

the Code clearly states that it is sufficient if the oratory be open to the faithful at least at the time of divine services, for it is not necessary even for a church to be open at all times. What divine services are meant in canon 1188? No definition can be found in the Code that is directly applicable here; however, canon 2256, § 1, states: "In canonibus qui sequuntur: Nomine divinorum officiorum intelliguntur functiones potestatis ordinis, quae de instituto Christi vel Ecclesiae ad divinum cultum ordinantur et a solis clericis fieri queunt"—and by analogy this definition can be invoked in the interpretation of canon 1188.[24] Hence at least during the time of such divine services, the faithful have the right to be present in a public oratory.

The Code states that the right of the faithful must be legitimately established, that is, it must be lawfully proved—"jus legitime comprobatum." This right can be proved in various ways of which the following are the most important: 1) An authentic document of the local Ordinary issued at the time of the erection, consecration, or blessing of the oratory, or subsequent thereto, declaring it to be public. 2) A legally valid document wherein the founder or proprietor of the oratory obligated himself to allow the faithful to use the oratory. 3) The erection or possession of a baptismal font in the oratory in accordance with canon 774, § 2. 4) Proof that the faithful acquired the right to use the oratory through lawful prescription. But even though it can be shown that the faithful have acquired this right, this fact alone does not make the oratory a public oratory, nor consequently, grant it the rights thereof, as the authorization of the local Ordinary is required to change its canonical status. Indications but by no means conclusive proofs that an oratory is public, and, therefore, open to the faithful, are the possession of a title, fixed altar, endowment, public entrance, campanile, etc. These factors, emphasized in former centuries,[25] afford very slight evidence to-

[24] Blat, *Commentarium,* IV, n. 40.

[25] Cf. above, Chapter IV.

day, as any or all of them may be possessed by an oratory which is nevertheless only semi-public. It is evident that until the faithful are disturbed in their use of an oratory, no legal proof need be afforded of their right to frequent it, legal proof becoming necessary only when the right is questioned or denied by the competent persons. The right of the faithful thus far has been considered only in its relation to the persons for whose convenience the public oratory primarily was erected. The question whether or not this right can be urged also against the local Ordinary, or in other words, whether or not he can lawfully restrict the free exercise of this right of the faithful, will be referred to in the next chapter.

Semi-public oratories are those erected for the convenience of a certain community or group of faithful who assemble there, but to which the other faithful have not the right of free access. The element that is stressed in this definition is the fact that the community or group of faithful in whose behalf the oratory is erected have the *exclusive right* to its use. Other persons have no right whatsoever to frequent it; if they are admitted, it is a mere favor which can be withdrawn at will. As this element has been sufficiently emphasized, only a few incidentals need yet be mentioned.

A semi-public oratory may be erected for the convenience of either a community or of a group of faithful—"communitatis vel coetus fidelium." The term "communitatis" here designates the persons resident in or pertaining to an institution; it, therefore, implies the existence of a moral person, ecclesiastical or civil. The term "coetus fidelium" designates only a number of physical persons without the further implication of an underlying moral person. That the community for whom the semi-public oratory is erected need not be a Religious community is evident both from the definition of a semi-public oratory and from canon 1192, § 4, which legislates for semi-public oratories erected in educational institutions, hospitals, prisons, barracks of soldiers, etc. The

Congregation of Rites on October 18, 1901, in a particular response stated that the term "coetus fidelium" as found in its general decree of 1899 (whence the Code derives it) can be understood "De quibuscumque fidelibus qui, assentiente domino loci et Ordinarii auctoritate interveniente, accedant ad praedicta oratoria pro audienda missa etiam ad adimplementum praecepti festivi."[26] The fact that the assent of the proprietor is required retains for the oratory its character of a semi-public oratory. However, it is in oratories of this type that many parishes had their origin, examples of which can be found in not a few of the rural parishes of our country.

The wording of the Code seems to imply that the semi-public oratory must be *erected* for the convenience of a community or group of faithful. Nevertheless, authors[27] consider that oratory to be semi-public which originally indeed was erected for the benefit of a private family or of a private individual, but subsequently by the authorization of the local Ordinary was destined for the use of a certain community or group of faithful. For such an oratory is not public, as not all the faithful have the right to frequent it; but neither is it now only private, as it no longer benefits merely a private family or individual; the only alternative is that it be considered as semi-public, its original status having been officially changed.[28]

Oratories that have been erected on ships and that have a permanent location are enumerated by A Coronata among semi-public oratories. The only argument he offers is a decision of the Congregation of Rites which he does not quote directly and the substance of which he gives incorrectly. On March 4, 1901, this Congregation published the following inquiry and response: "Utrum cappellae navium aut altaria in ipsis navibus erecta pro

---

26 This decree is not found in an authentic collection but is quoted by Vermeersch-Creusen, *Epitome,* II, n. 498, and by Cocchi, *Commentarium,* V, n. 29.

27 Cf. A Coronata, *De Locis et Temp. Sacris,* n. 76; Vermeersch-Creusen, *Epitome,* II, n. 498.

28 "Mutatis mutandis," this can be applied also to the other two classes of oratories.

Sacro litando debeant considerari ut oratoria privata vel publica?—Si cappella locum fixum habeat in navi, uti publica habenda est: secus neque publica est, neque privata, sed habetur uti altare portatile."[29] Referring to this decision (but not quoting it) A Coronata writes "Qua (decisione) tamen dicitur simpliciter, has cappellas esse publicas pro navigantibus, seu aliis verbis, semi-publicas, quia destinantur determinato coetui personarum."[30] The wording of the decision, however, does not justify such a statement as it clearly calls these oratories public, and they are so considered by Many,[31] Vermeersch-Creusen,[32] Cocchi,[33] Blat[34] and Bouuaert-Simenon.[35]

Finally, a **private oratory** is one erected in a private house for the convenience of some family or of a private individual. As such oratories usually are erected in private homes and are destined exclusively for private use, they are known also as domestic oratories,[36] though the term domestic oratory is less extensive than private oratory. It is evident that the faithful in general do not enjoy the right of frequenting a private oratory since this right is denied them as a strict right even in the case of a semi-public oratory.

The term "familiae" as used in the Code's definition must be understood in its natural and usual meaning; it, therefore, excludes corporations or moral persons whose physical members are sometimes referred to collectively as a family. Commenting on this term, Augustine writes: "But it includes all the inhabitants of a house living under the authority of the same *paterfamilias*."[37] Even this interpretation, however, is too extensive, for it includes all the servants residing in the house, whereas

29 § 5; D. A., 4069.
30 *De Locis et Temp. Sacris*, n. 77.
31 *De Locis Sacris*, n. 70.
32 *Epitome*, II, n. 498.
33 *Commentarium*, V, n. 29.
34 *Commentarium*, IV, n. 40.
35 *Manuale*, n. 787, note 3.
36 Some, however, as will be shown presently, are not erected in private homes and consequently should not be called domestic oratories.
37 *Commentary*, VI, 68.

only those servants whose presence is required at the holy Sacrifice participate in all the advantages arising from a private oratory, and these servants alone can be understood as forming part of the family for whose convenience the private oratory is erected. But this matter was examined in Chapter VI and will be referred to again later.

To obviate all doubts concerning the status of the oratories of cardinals and bishops, the Code expressly and clearly states:

Oratoria S. R. E. Cardinalium et Episcoporum sive residentialium sive titularium, licet privata, fruuntur tamen omnibus iuribus et privilegiis quibus oratoria semi-publica gaudent (can. 1189).

These oratories, therefore, are private; nevertheless they enjoy all the rights and privileges of semi-public oratories. The reason the Code devotes a special canon to them is not only to safeguard the privileges which they have long enjoyed,[38] but also because if it had not expressly stated that they are private oratories, they would not have been so considered. For the Code in declaring that private oratories are such as are erected in private houses, etc., would have been interpreted as thereby excluding the oratories of cardinals and bishops, since it was declared by Benedict XIV[39]—and has been maintained ever since—that the houses of these dignitaries were not private houses. These oratories, therefore, constitute a distinct species of private oratories in as far as: 1) they are not erected in private houses; 2) they enjoy the rights and privileges of semi-public oratories. They are private rather than domestic oratories.

---

38 E. g., the privilege that in these oratories any of the faithful could fulfil the obligation of a preceptive Mass—a privilege that had been recognized by the Congregation of Rites, July 2, 1661; D. A., 1196.

39 Ep. encycl. *"Magno cum,"* July 2, 1751, § 2; Fontes, 413.

What may well be considered as another special class of private oratories is referred to in canon 1190:

Aediculae in coemeterio a familiis seu personis privatis ad suam sepulturam erectae, sunt oratoria privata.

Also these oratories are not domestic in the strict sense of the term for they are erected in a public place (a cemetery), not in private homes; moreover, as will be seen, they enjoy, or at least can be given more extensive rights than the usual private oratories. Nevertheless, the Code considers them private as they are erected by private persons for their own sepulture. Cemetery chapels of this type, though somewhat numerous in Europe,[40] are extremely rare in our country. The chapels that usually are erected in our cemeteries are not private but public (cemetery) chapels; they are erected and intended not for a single private person or family, but for all the faithful of the locality in which the cemetery is situated, as well as for any other faithful who may visit it. Such chapels are erected either directly by the local Ordinary or by the municipal authorities or cemetery corporation with the permission of the local Ordinary; they are public oratories in the strict sense of the term as defined by canon 1188, § 2, 1°, and, therefore, must be distinguished from the private cemetery chapels of canon 1190. Finally, cemetery chapels that are neither public nor private but semi-public, and, therefore, to be distinguished from both of the above classes, are those pertaining to a Religious community.[41]

Private oratories, therefore, may be sub-divided into three classes: 1) Oratories erected in private homes for the convenience of a family or of private individuals; these are domestic oratories in the strict sense of the term. 2) Private oratories of cardinals or bishops. 3) Private oratories erected in cemeteries. Such a sub-division finds justification not only in the fact that it is im-

---

40 Cf. Brehm, *Synopsis*, p. 201; Vermeersch-Creusen, *Epitome*, II, n. 499.

41 Cf. Barin, *Commentarium*, *Eph. Liturg.*, XL (1926), 62.

plied in the Code, but also and especially in the different privileges that these various classes of oratories enjoy by the law of the Code or can be granted by the concession of the local Ordinary.

CHAPTER VIII.

The Laws Governing Public Oratories.

Oratoria publica eodem iure quo ecclesiae reguntur (can. 1191, § 1).

In these few words the Code applies to public oratories all the laws that govern churches. It, therefore, necessitates at least a summary investigation of these laws, the most important of which are given in Book III, Title IX, Canons 1161-1187. Although public oratories are not mentioned once in the twenty-seven canons of this title which is expressly and immediately legislating for churches, nevertheless in virtue of the unequivocal prescription of canon 1191, § 1, these canons must be understood as legislating also for public oratories.[1] Hence, as Blat pertinently remarks: "Significatio iuridica verbi ecclesia (in can. 1162-1187) comprehendit dicta oratoria."[2] This point is emphasized here in order to avoid the necessity of referring constantly to canon 1191 as justification for applying to public oratories canons that apparently are concerned solely with churches. In citing or paraphrasing these canons the term public oratory will be substituted freely for the word church, as these canons are of interest here only because they are laws governing public oratories.

The legislation on public oratories will be examined in five articles under the captions: 1) Erection. 2) Dedication. 3) Violation and Reconciliation. 4) Divine Services that may be celebrated. 5) Miscellanea.

---

1 Naturally, if the context or the nature of a canon in whole or in part excludes its application to public oratories, to attempt such application would be absurd. Thus, can. 1161, the first canon of Title IX, gives a definition of a church; it is evident that this definition is not to be applied to public oratories which are defined in can. 1188. It likewise is patent that regulations referring exclusively to a certain class of churches, e.g., to cathedral churches or to parish churches, are not to be applied to public oratories.

2 *Commentarium,* IV, n. 43.

Article 1: Erection of Public Oratories.

No public oratory may be erected without the express and written consent of the local Ordinary;[3] though the Vicar General is a local Ordinary,[4] he is not competent to grant this permission unless empowered to do so by a special mandate (can. 1162, § 1). If the Vicar General is thus empowered, he grants the necessary permission as a mere mandatary of the person whose Vicar General he is and not as a local Ordinary. In demanding the consent of the local Ordinary this law presents no difficulties and offers no departure from the pre-Code law,[5] except in as far as it demands that this consent be given in writing; it, therefore, needs no commentary.

This written consent of the local Ordinary is required even if there is question of a public oratory of Religious. Though it is true that the permission granted to clerical Religious to erect a Religious house implies also the right of having a church or public oratory annexed to that house (can. 497, § 2), nevertheless, a special written permission is required before this church or oratory may be erected in a certain and definite location. Not even the privilege of exemption frees Religious from the observance of this law (can. 497, § 2, and 1162, § 4).

Before granting his consent, the local Ordinary must consult the rectors of neighboring churches in order to be able the better to determine whether the erection of the new oratory will be detrimental to their churches without offering the faithful a spiritual benefit proportionate to the injury it occasions (can. 1162, § 3). If the Ordinary grants permission to erect the oratory despite

---

3 This consent likewise is required if a private or semi-public oratory is to be changed into a public oratory. Cf. Barin, *Commentarium*, *Eph. Liturg.*, XXXIX (1925), 374.

4 As local Ordinaries can. 198 enumerates residential bishops, abbots *nullius*, prelates *nullius*, their Vicars General, Apostolic Administrators, Vicars Apostolic, Prefects Apostolic and those persons who, by law or approved constitutions, are their "ad interim" successors. The major Superiors of exempt clerical Religious are Ordinaries, but not local Ordinaries.

5 Cf. above, Chapter V, Article 2, and Chapter VI, Article 1.

the adverse counsel of these rectors,[6] they have—collectively or individually—the right to institute an action in the ecclesiastical courts known as "novi operis nuntiatio" (can. 1162, § 3). When recourse is had to this legal action a mandate usually is issued suspending work on the new oratory until the rights of the interested parties are defined by a judicial sentence (can. 1676). A similar mandate in modern civil law is known as a preventive injunction.[7]

The Ordinary is forbidden to allow the erection of a public oratory if he foresees that there will not be the necessary means to provide for its completion and preservation and also for the support of its priest (if it is to have one regularly) and the defrayal of the other expenditures incidental to conducting religious worship (can. 1162, § 2). Among these means are to be computed not only the income from an invested capital, but also any other source of revenue which the oratory may enjoy or probably will obtain in the future. If an oratory is to serve as a succursal chapel for a large parish, or if it is erected in connection with a Religious house, its necessary financial means are presumed thereby to be assured;[8] likewise, if the founder or patron of the oratory obligates himself to furnish all the necessary means, such assurance is deemed sufficient, at least in the case of an oratory that is not to be consecrated.[9] In all instances, however, the final decision as to the adequacy of the resources or their guarantee rests with the local Ordinary. He, likewise, should refuse permission for the erection of a public oratory if there is a probable danger that it will be used for profane purposes (can. 1165, § 2); lack of sufficient revenue is only one of the indications of such danger, though it probably is the most frequent.

---

6 This he may lawfully do, for, though he is obliged to consult them, he need not follow even their unanimous advice if, in his judgment, it would be better to disregard that advice (can. 105, § 1).

7 Cf. Pomeroy, *Equity Jurisprudence*, I, n. 3.

8 Cf. Reiffenstuel, *Jus Canonicum Univers.*, tom. 3, Tit. 48, § 1, n. 10; Barin, *Commentarium, Eph. Liturg.*, XXXIX (1925), 374.

9 Cf. Many, *De Locis Sacris*, n. 71.

In the erection (or restoration) of public oratories the Ordinaries shall provide for the observance of the Christian traditions of ecclesiastical architecture and the laws of sacred art; to secure the laudable end intended by this law, experts in ecclesiastical architecture should be consulted whenever necessary (can. 1164, § 1). In many dioceses a permanent building committee has been appointed which carefully examines the plans for any sacred edifice that is to be erected in the diocese. Such committees are not prescribed by the Code, yet in view of some of the "architectural monstrosities" that have been permitted at times in our ecclesiastical buildings, they seem very desirable. That the Ordinary has the right and the duty to reject plans that are unbecoming for a place of divine worship cannot be questioned.[10] The above law is quite general, and the attainment of its end—the erection of sacred edifices worthy of the high purpose to which they are destined—will depend largely on the discerning taste of those who are to enforce it.

Of a more specific nature is the only other prescription which the Code offers concerning the material structure of a sacred edifice: "In ecclesia nullus aperiatur aditus vel fenestra ad laicorum domus" (can. 1164, § 2). Apropos to this canon it is to be noted that the Code does not prohibit an entrance (or window) from a Religious house or priest's residence, but forbids only such as are from the homes of the laity. Moreover, although it would seem certain that also this law must be applied in all its rigor to public oratories in virtue of the general norm of canon 1191, § 1, nevertheless the necessity of such application is questioned by several commentators of the Code, notably by Barin: "Sane si Codex in notione oratorii publici illud efficit *in commodum privatae personae* (vel collegii) praesertim erectum, videtur non urgere tam stricte pro oratoriis observantiam can. 1164, § 2; esset enim saepe incommodus ingressus per ianuam in via publica. Adde, talem privatum aditum vel prospectum quan-

[10] Cf. Bouuaert-Simenon, *Manuale*, n. 770; Woywod, *Commentary*, II, n. 1202.

doque necessarium esse pro custodia ipsius oratorii."[11] The argument from the primary purpose of a public oratory is by no means weak. Without entering into the reasons for his view, A Coronata asserts: "Ex certa lege generali probari nequit in oratorio publico privatum ostium aut fenestram sicut in ecclesiis prohiberi, nisi in casibus specialibus aliud praescribant sive Ordinarius loci erectionem oratorii permittens, sive S. Congregatio."[12] In a practical case (which will not arise very frequently, at least not in our country) the ruling of the Ordinary would have to be observed who would not seem to be exceeding his power[13] in allowing or forbidding an entrance from a layman's home into a public oratory.[14]

Finally it is the right of the local Ordinary to bless and lay the corner stone of a public oratory; if, however, the oratory belongs to exempt clerical Religious, their major Superior has this right. Either Ordinary can delegate a priest for this ceremony (can. 1163 and 1156). The Pontifical[15] contains the rite to be used if a bishop officiates, while the Ritual[16] gives the rite to be used by a priest. If holy Mass is celebrated at the conclusion of the ceremony, it is to be a solemn votive Mass[17] of the Divine Person, Mystery or Saint[18] in whose special honor the oratory is erected. Although A Coronata[19] denies that there is a strict obligation to have the blessing of the corner stone for an oratory (and Vermeersch-Creusen[20] cite this opinion, without, however, approving

---

11 *Commentarium, Eph. Liturg.*, XXXIX (1925), 376.

12 *De Locis et Temp. Sacris*, n. 75.

13 In virtue of can. 15.

14 Such entrances were the subjects of even greater controversies under the old law; cf. Mostazo, *De Causis Piis*, L. 5, c. 10, n. 11 sq.; De Bonis, *De Oratoriis Pub.*, n. 21 sq. and 344 sq.

15 Pars II, *De Benedictione et Impositione Primarii Lapidis.*

16 Tit. 8, c. 26, *Ritus Benedicendi et Imponendi Primarium Lapidem.*

17 Cf. *Missale Romanum, Additiones et Variationes in Rubricis Missalis*, Tit. 2, n. 9.

18 Persons beatified but not yet canonized cannot be chosen as patrons without an Apostolic indult (can. 1168, §3).

19 *De Locis et Temp. Sacris*, n. 73, 3°.

20 *Epitome*, II, n. 500.

or rejecting it), nevertheless, if at all possible [21] this beautiful rite with its inspiring prayers should not be omitted.

Article 2: The Dedication of Public Oratories.

Dedication is a sacred rite instituted by the Church in virtue of which a profane place is rendered sacred and is perpetually destined to divine worship by a lawful minister.[22] If the rite is solemnly administered, it is called consecration or solemn dedication, otherwise it is known as simple dedication or blessing. The Pontifical [23] contains the rite of consecration, the Ritual [24] that of blessing. Though these rites differ as sacramentals, their canonical effects are identical; both render a hitherto profane place sacred with all the consequences that this implies. In the dedication of places to divine worship the prescriptions of the approved liturgical books must be observed (can. 2 and 1154).

The consecration or solemn dedication of a public oratory is not prescribed; in all instances, however, it is permitted unless the oratory is constructed of wood, iron or some other metal (can. 1165, §§ 3, 4, and 1191, § 2). The more general practice observed in recent times is not to consecrate an oratory unless there is some special reason urging its consecration.[25] If not consecrated, a public oratory must be blessed, otherwise sacred functions cannot be celebrated therein (can. 1191, § 2, and 1165, § 1). The blessing in question is not the ordinary "Benedictio loci vel domus" [26] which will suffice for a semi-public or private oratory (can. 1196), but the special constitutive blessing referred to above whereby a church

---

21 It is evidently impossible when an already existing private or semi-public oratory is converted into a public oratory.

22 Cf. Wernz, *Jus Decretalium*, tom. 3, n. 436; also can. 1154 and 1191.

23 Pars II, *De Ecclesiae Dedicatione seu Consecratione.*

24 Tit. 8, c. 27, *Ritus Benedicendi Novam Ecclesiam seu Oratorium Publicum.*

25 E. g., its antiquity, its unusual size or architectural beauty, the fact that it is a place of pilgrimage frequented by very many of the faithful, etc.

26 *Rituale Romanum,* Tit. 8, c. 6.

or oratory is perpetually dedicated to the service of God (can. 1191, § 2).

If a further proof for the necessity of at least blessing a public oratory is needed, it can be found in canon 822, § 1, which states: "Missa celebranda est . . . in ecclesia vel oratorio consecrato aut benedicto ad normam iuris, salvo praescripto can. 1196." But canon 1196 admits that domestic or semi-public oratories alone need be neither consecrated nor blessed. In his treatise on the obligation of at least blessing public oratories, Many writes: "—1) Sicubi existat consuetudo non benedicendi oratoria publica, praesertim minoris momenti, ita tamen ut ad normam conc. Trid. episcopus ea designet, visitet et cultui divino exclusive addicat, haec consuetudo non videtur illegitima.—2) In omni casu, episcopus *ad tempus,* donec expectetur opportunitas benedictionis, in his oratoriis permittere potest missae celebrationem." [27] Vermeersch-Creusen [28] and A Coronata [29] cite and apparently accept these opinions, the second of which certainly is correct in virtue of the power which the Ordinary enjoys of allowing Mass even "Extra ecclesiam et oratorium . . . . iusta ac rationabili de causa, in aliquo extraordinario casu et per modum actus" (can. 822, § 4). As to the first opinion, however the existence of such a custom is no longer likely, and if it does exist anywhere, its force would have to be judged according to the general principles on customs as enunciated in the Code (can. 5, 25-30).

The minister for the consecration of a public oratory, even though it pertains to Regulars, is the local Ordinary in whose territory the oratory is erected, provided he has the episcopal character; but even if devoid of the episcopal character, he may give permission to perform

27 *De Locis Sacris,* n. 72.

28 *Epitome,* II, n. 500.

29 *De Locis et Temp. Sacris,* n. 73, 4°.

the consecration to any bishop [30] of his own rite. The Vicar General, however, even if a (titular) bishop, can neither perform the consecration nor give the necessary permission to another unless he has a special mandate to that effect (can. 1155). The minister for the blessing of a public oratory is likewise the local Ordinary in whose territory the oratory is situated; if, however, the oratory pertains to exempt clerical Religious, their major Superior has the right to bless it. Either Ordinary can commission a priest to perform the blessing (can. 1156). It is to be noted that the limitation of the power of the Vicar General made above is not repeated in this law on the blessing of an oratory; consequently, unless restricted by the special reservation or by the will of the bishop, he participates in the rights conceded by this canon.[31] Notwithstanding any privilege to the contrary, no one may consecrate or bless an oratory without the consent of the Ordinary who possesses these respective rights as determined in the above canons (can. 1157).

The consecration or blessing of a public oratory is not limited to any special day, though the Code states that it is more becoming to select a Sunday or holy day of obligation for the consecration (can. 1166, § 1). The consecrating bishop, as well as the petitioners [32] for the consecration of the oratory, must observe the day preceding as a day of fast [33] (can. 1166, § 2). The consecrating prelate may grant an indulgence of one year to those who visit the oratory on the day of its consecration; to those who will visit it on the anniversary day he may grant an indulgence of fifty days if he is a bishop, of a hundred days if an archbishop and of two hundred days if a cardinal (can. 1166, § 3). Together with the oratory

---

30 And to a cardinal even though he is not a bishop in virtue of a special privilege conceded cardinals in can. 239, § 1, 20°. Cf. Augustine (*Commentary*, VI, 4) and A Coronata (*De Locis et Temp. Sacris*, n. 5, 3°) who erroneously imply that a cardinal can be delegated to perform the consecration only if he is a bishop.

31 Cf. can. 198, 368 and 369.

32 For the controversy on the extent of this term, cf. Vermeersch-Creusen, *Epitome*, II, n. 483.

33 But not as a day of fast and abstinence; cf. can. 1251 sq.

its principal altar—or if this already is consecrated, a secondary one—must be consecrated (can. 1165, § 5). Neither the obligation of the fast, nor the concession of the indulgences, nor the necessity of consecrating an altar are applicable if the oratory is only blessed.

After the dedication of an oratory its titular feast [34] must be celebrated annually in the manner prescribed by the laws of liturgy, and if it was consecrated, the anniversary of its consecration likewise must be celebrated (can. 1167 and 1168, § 2). Both feasts are Doubles of the First Class with an Octave. A thorough examination of the liturgical laws referred to in these canons will be found in the works of almost all recent liturgicians.[35]

An oratory does not lose its consecration [36] or blessing unless: 1) it is totally destroyed, or 2) the larger part of the walls has collapsed, or 3) it has been reduced to profane use by the local Ordinary (can. 1170). The first two exceptions given in this canon may be considered as generalizations of numerous decisions in particular cases issued by the Congregation of Rites;[37] for if these decisions had been issued after the Code, they would have been viewed as natural applications of the general principles given in the Code to specific cases. The strictly liturgical prescriptions of these decrees (e. g., the obligation of replacing any of the twelve crosses erected at the consecration whenever they have been destroyed), though not expressly referred to in the Code, remain in force in virtue of the general norm given in canon 2.

---

34 The proper title or name by which the oratory is known is selected prior to the blessing of the cornerstone as it is used in that ceremony as well as in the actual dedication. Although can. 1168, § 1, prohibits the changing of the title *after* the dedication, it would seem at least unbecoming to change it even prior thereto unless urged by a weighty reason.

35 E. g., Wuest-Mullaney, *Matters Liturgical*, n. 726 sq.; Wapelhorst, *Compendium*, n. 248 sq.; Martinucci-Menghini, *Manuale*, L. 7, Tit. 2, c. 3; Brehm, *Synopsis*, p. 136 sq.

36 Unfortunately, usually only the loss of consecration is referred to as execration; it would be convenient if this term included also the loss of blessing.

37 The more recent of these decisions were issued March 11, 1871; Aug. 31, 1872; Sept. 4, 1875; July 13, 1883; Jan. 16, 1886; May 19, 1896; Aug. 9, 1897; D. A., 3240, 3269, 3372, 3584, 3651, 3907, 3962.

The third cause for the loss of consecration or blessing, the reduction of an oratory to profane use, is explained in canon 1187: "Si qua ecclesia [oratorium publicum] nullo modo ad cultum divinum adhiberi possit et omnes aditus interclusi sint ad eam reficiendam, in usum profanum non sordidum ab Ordinario loci redigi potest, et onera cum reditibus titulusque paroeciae, si ecclesia sit paroecialis, in aliam ecclesiam ab eodem Ordinario transferantur."[38] If, therefore, the oratory was reduced to profane use without the consent of the local Ordinary (e. g., by the civil authorities), it thereby might be violated,[39] but it would not lose its consecration or blessing (can. 1170 and 1187). Before the Code it was necessary to demolish the sacred edifice, the materials of which could then be used for profane purposes; the Code allows the building itself to be so used if the conditions of the above canon are verified. The impossibility of repairing the edifice may be due to an absolute lack of funds for making the necessary but yet possible repairs, or to the fact that even though the funds are now available, the building is so dilapidated that an entirely new structure is necessary, mere repair no longer being possible. The transfer of the title is prescribed only for parish churches, but the transfer of obligations with their revenue (e. g., foundation Masses) must be applied also to public oratories.

That the Code most earnestly deprecates the reduction of a dedicated oratory to profane use is evident not only from the strong wording of this canon (and the obligation imposed by canon 1186 on various persons to make all necessary repairs), but also from the prescriptions of canons 1162, § 2, and 1165, § 2, whereby the Ordinary is forbidden to allow the erection of a public oratory, and especially its dedication, if there is danger that in the course of time it will be used for profane purposes. These canons are intended as means of averting

---

38 Compare this canon with that of the Council of Trent, Sess. XXI, *de Ref.*, c. 7.

39 Cf. can. 1172 and the next article of this chapter.

both the unlawful reduction of an oratory to profane purposes by unauthorized agents and also its canonical reduction to such purposes by the local Ordinary; for even the lawful departure from the literal observance of the old axiom of law, "Semel Deo dedicatum non est ad usus humanos ulterius transferendum,"[40] is a reluctant concession to be used only as a last resource.

Article 3: The Violation and Reconciliation of Public Oratories.

As the Code does not give a definition of either of these terms canonists formulate their own definitions. Bouuaert-Simenon define the violation[41] of a sacred place as "Contaminatio eius sanctitatis, propter aliquos actus graviter injuriosos, in iure determinatos, ita ut jam divino cultui non sit apta nisi prius reconcilietur. Vocari posset etiam temporalis et determinata suspensio effectuum consecrationis aut benedictionis;"[42] and by Vermeersch-Creusen as "Impietas seu peccatum quod, iudice auctoritate ecclesiastica, ita ipsum locum afficere censetur, ut, quamvis sacer maneat, decenti sacrarum functionum celebrationi ante expiationem aptus non existimetur."[43] Its reconciliation is defined by Cocchi as "Actus quo ecclesia [oratorium] polluta a macula, per indignam actionem contracta, purgatur et divino cultui restituitur;"[44] and by A Coronata as "Ritus sacer quo ecclesia violata divino cultui restituitur."[45] It may be advisable to add that the canonists of today are almost unanimous in admitting the possibility of violation only in churches or oratories that have been dedicated—a matter long under controversy.[46] Hence there would be no obligation to

---

40 R. J. 51 in VI.

41 Though the term execration (as was mentioned above) is used almost exclusively in reference to a consecrated place and not to one merely blessed, the term desecration is used for the violation of either a consecrated or a blessed place.

42 *Manuale*, n. 779.

43 *Epitome*, II, n. 489.

44 *Commentarium*, V, n. 19.

45 *De Locis et Temp. Sacris*, n. 30.

46 Cf. Gasparri, *De SS. Eucharistia*, I, n. 247; Many, *De Locis Sacris*, n. 39; Vermeersch-Creusen, *Epitome*, II, n. 489.

reconcile an undedicated oratory even though all the other conditions requisite for violation were present.

A public oratory is violated by any one or several of the following acts, provided they are certain, notorious and were committed in the oratory itself: 1) The crime of homicide; 2) Injurious and grave shedding of blood; 3) Impious and sordid use to which the oratory has been addicted; 4) The burial of the corpse of an infidel or of an excommunicated person against whom there was issued a declaratory or condemnatory sentence of excommunication (can. 1172, § 1). As the laws concerning the violation of a sacred place restrict the free exercise of rights (the celebration of divine services) they must be interpreted strictly (can. 19), for "Odiosa sunt restringenda." [47] Using this principle of interpretation, the following conclusions are evident:

The four kinds of acts enumerated, and they alone, cause the violation of an oratory.[48] To cause violation they must be *certain*: if, therefore, there is any doubt concerning them, either a doubt of law or of fact, the oratory is not violated. They must be *notorious*: in canon 2197 the Code defines the two species of notoriety (notoriety by law and notoriety in fact) and these definitions can be applied in interpreting this canon. The acts must be perpetrated *in the oratory itself*: hence, if they occur in an adjoining room (even if it is the sacristy), or in the vestibule, or on the roof, or in the belfry, the oratory is not violated.[49]

---

[47] Cf. R. J. 15 in VI.

[48] Can. 1172, § 2 adds that a cemetery is not violated by the fact that the church (oratory) to which it is contiguous is violated, or vice versa. Though this is implied in § 1 of can. 1172, together with can. 1207, the Code expressly mentions it as the old law (c. un., *de consecratione ecclesiae*, III, 21, in VI) declared that an adjoining cemetery was violated by the violation of the church, though it did not admit that the church was violated by the mere violation of the cemetery.

[49] Among the other applications made, the following may be mentioned: A church (oratory) is not violated if a person outside the church is murdered by a person within the church, and, according to a few authors, not even if a person within is murdered by a person outside the church; this second opinion, however, is rejected by most authors. Cf. Barbosa, *Jus Eccl. Univers.*, L. 2, c. 4; Many, *De Locis Sacris*, n. 31, 38; A Coronata, *De Locis et Temp. Sacris*, n. 28, 2°.

Not any homicide violates the oratory, but the crime of homicide— "delictum homicidii"—which presupposes grave guilt.[50] Hence homicide committed in justifiable self-defense or by a morally irresponsible person would not cause violation. Gasparri[51] and Augustine[52] claim that the execution of a just sentence of capital punishment by the lawful authorities is to be included here; this view, however, must be rejected, for such an execution could not be called a *crime* of homicide. Whether it would nevertheless cause violation because the oratory would thereby be diverted to sordid and impious use will be seen presently. A morally imputable suicide, however, is included here even by those canonists who advert to the fact that a strict interpretation of the word homicide does not include suicide. The reason they offer for departing from strict interpretation in this one instance is that the old law,[53] identical with the new in this particular, was so understood despite the fact that it, too, was supposed to have been strictly interpreted. Hence, applying canon 6, also the Code law must be understood as including suicide.

The shedding of blood that causes violation must be grave, injurious or unjust, and there must be a real effusion of blood in some quantity, or as the authors say, a copious shedding. Hence, if accidental, slight, or self inflicted but not fatal, it would not cause violation. That the shedding of human blood alone is referred to is evident from the use of the word injurious or unjust. Both the serious irreverence offered to the sacred place and the gravity of the injury inflicted on the person are implied in the addition of the word grave.

The third cause is rather general, and unfortunately, the Code nowhere defines what is meant by impious or sordid use. Concerning the meaning of these terms Barin writes: "*Impius* dicitur usus propter contrarietatem

---

50 Cf. can. 2195; § 1; cf. also can. 2350 and 2354.

51 *De SS. Eucharistia,* I, n. 250.

52 *Commentary,* VI, 37.

53 C. 4, X, *de consecratione ecclesiae,* III, 40.

religioni; *sordidus* etsi non peccaminosus, propter indecentiam."[54] Some acts are considered by all men as impious, sordid or both; they certainly would violate the oratory. Concerning other acts whose nature is not so evident, there could exist reasonable doubt, and consequently, when such a doubt exists, the oratory is to be considered as not violated. Many authors[55] declare that the words "usus" and "addicta" insinuate the necessity of the act being customary, repeated or at least of some duration. There is at least some intrinsic probability to this view in addition to the extrinsic probability afforded by the authority of the authors who defend it. Hence, a single and brief impious or sordid act could be considered, at least, as a doubtful case of violation and, therefore, as no violation, for the act must be certain in law and in fact. Applying this to the question of the infliction of capital punishment referred to above, it would seem that one would have to conclude that it would not violate the oratory. This conclusion nevertheless is categorically denied by Vermeersch-Creusen[56] who, however, do not avail themselves of the argument based on the words "usus" and "addicta."

The last cause is more specific and consequently is liable to less doubt. By burial, in canon 1172, is meant only the actual interment or sepulture of the corpse; the other parts of an ecclesiastical funeral as enumerated in canon 1204 (the transfer of the corpse to the church with the accompanying prayers and the exequial services in the church) are neither required nor alone will suffice to cause violation. The term infidel must be limited to persons who have not been baptized; and from unbaptized persons cathechumens must be excluded in virtue of canon 1239, § 2, and probably also the unbaptized infants of at least Catholic parents in virtue of the common

---

[54] *Commentarium, Eph. Liturg.*, XXXVIII (1924), 236.

[55] Bouuaert-Simenon, *Manuale*, n. 779; Cocchi, *Commentarium*, V, n. 17; A Coronata, *De Locis et Temp. Sacris*, n. 28; Barin, *Commentarium, Eph. Liturg.*, XXXVIII (1924), 236.

[56] *Epitome*, II, n. 489.

teaching of canonists. Finally, the sentences of excommunication referred to must be understood in the light of canons 1576, § 1 and 2257 sq. A Coronata[57] makes a strong plea to limit violation in this instance to the burial of the excommunicated who were "vitandi." This opinion is contrary to that of most commentators on the Code, though his argumentation is not without some force and the probability of his opinion is not denied by Vermeersch-Creusen[58] and Bouuaert-Simenon[59] who cite it. Although the burial of the persons above described alone violates the oratory, this does not imply that all other persons may be buried there; for canon 1205, § 2, forbids the burial in churches (and, therefore, in public[60] oratories by can. 1191, § 1) of all except royal personages, abbots and prelates *nullius*, residential bishops, cardinals and popes.

In an oratory that has been violated the celebration of the divine offices, the administration of the sacraments and the burial of the dead[61] are strictly prohibited until it has been reconciled (can. 1173, § 1). Divine offices are defined in canon 2256, § 1 as those functions of the power of orders which by the institution of Christ or the Church are ordained for divine worship and are performed exclusively by the clergy. Although this definition is intended for the canons subsequent to canon 2256, by analogy it can be invoked here.[62] If the violation occurs during the divine offices they must cease immediately. Even holy Mass must be discontinued if the violation oc-

---

57 *De Locis et Temp. Sacris*, n. 28.

58 *Epitome*, II, n. 489, d.

59 *Manuale*, n. 779.

60 That the burial of the faithful is forbidden in any oratory (except private cemetery chapels expressly erected by the faithful for their own sepulture according to can. 1190, and the semi-public cemetery chapels of Religious) is evident also from can. 1205, § 1, which commands their burial in a blessed cemetery.

61 This term cannot be restricted here to the actual interment as was done above, but includes the usual exequial services held in church, as they also are divine offices.

62 As was done also in Chapter VII, Article 2, 1.

curs before the Canon of the Mass or after Communion;[63] if, however, it occurs during the Canon of the Mass the priest shall continue the Mass until Communion, that is, until he has consumed the Sacred Species (can. 1173, § 2).

An oratory that has been violated must be reconciled as soon as possible according to the rites prescribed in the approved liturgical books (can. 1174, § 1). If, however, the oratory was violated by the burial of the corpse of an infidel or of an excommunicated person, the corpse must first be removed if this can be done without grave inconvenience (can. 1175). The obligation of reconciling sacred places as soon as possible is a grave one, nor does the Code distinguish between such as are used daily for divine services and those which are used only a few times a year. All are sacred places and, therefore, the stain inflicted upon them by violation must be effaced as quickly as possible. But there is an obligation only when the violation is certain; if it is only doubtful, a provisional (*ad cautelam*) reconciliation may be made, even though this is not obligatory (can. 1174, § 2). The reconciliation must be effected according to the rites prescribed in the Pontifical [64] and in the Ritual [65] for consecrated and blessed churches respectively.[66] Ordinary holy water may be used in reconciling a blessed oratory, but for a consecrated oratory water blessed for this special purpose according to the laws of liturgy must be used. He who reconciles a consecrated oratory can bless this water even though he is not a bishop (can. 1177). The Code expressly mentions that this water need not be blessed by a bishop because the Congregation of Rites [67] had declared

63 Cf. *Missale Romanum, De Defectibus,* Tit. 10, n. 2, which must be corrected in virtue of this canon.

64 Pars II, *De Ecclesiae et Coemeterii Reconciliatione.*

65 Tit. 8, c. 28, *Ritus Reconciliandi Ecclesiam Violatam quae fuerit tantummodo benedicta.*

66 The Congregation of Rites on Aug. 19, 1634, declared that even if holy Mass had been celebrated in good faith in a violated church it thereby was not reconciled; D. A., 611.

67 June 20, 1626, and March 13, 1821; D. A., 411 and 2612.

that even if a priest commissioned by the Holy See reconciled a consecrated church he was obliged to use water blessed for this purpose by a bishop.

The minister of reconciliation of a blessed oratory is its rector[68] or any other priest having at least his presumed consent. If the violated oratory was consecrated, the minister of its reconciliation is the local Ordinary unless it pertains to exempt clerical Religious whose major Superior will then have the right and duty to reconcile it. Both Ordinaries may delegate any priest to perform the ceremony. In cases of grave and urgent necessity, if the Ordinary cannot be approached, the rector of a consecrated oratory even though not delegated may perform the rite and later inform the Ordinary of the fact of its reconciliation (can. 1176 and 1156). Whether bishop or priest, he who reconciles a consecrated oratory must use the rite given in the Pontifical and not that of the Ritual. The faculties given in these canons are far more liberal than those of the old law. Formerly a blessed church or oratory could be reconciled only by the Ordinary or by a priest delegated by him; a consecrated church or oratory only by the Ordinary or a priest delegated by the Holy See.[69] In the more extensive faculties of the new law, the Code to a large extent removes one of the principal obstacles that delayed reconciliation, and thereby renders its restoration for divine worship more easy of attainment.

---

68 The chaplain or priest in charge of the oratory; justification for the use of the term rector can be found in can. 479, § 1 and 1191, § 1.

69 Cf. Many, *De Locis Sacris*, n. 42; Gasparri, *De SS. Eucharistia*, I, n. 256.

Article 4: Divine Services That May Be Celebrated in Public Oratories.

§ 1. Oratoria publica eodem iure quo ecclesiae reguntur.

§ 2. Quare in oratorio publico, dummodo auctoritate Ordinarii ad publicum Dei cultum perpetuo per benedictionem vel consecrationem, ad normam can. 1155, 1156, dedicatum fuerit, omnes sacrae functiones celebrari possunt, salvo contrario rubricarum praescripto (can. 1191).

A merely cursory reading of this canon might lead to the conclusion that the only limitations to the sacred functions that may be held in a dedicated public oratory are those defined by the laws of liturgy; but the first paragraph of the canon states that public oratories are governed by the same laws that govern churches, and as these laws reveal other limitations, they, too, must be observed. The principal canons in question here are 462, 481-483, 609, § 3, 716 and 1171. These canons declare that the parochial rights shall not be infringed upon nor the parochial ministry injured—principles that have been stressed for centuries.[70]

Canon 462 enumerates the functions reserved to pastors of which the following alone need be considered here, as the others [71] usually are not performed in a sacred place: "—1) Baptismum conferre sollemniter. —2) Sacras ordinationes et ineundas nuptias denuntiare; matrimoniis assistere, nuptialem benedictionem impertiri. —3) Iusta funebria persolvere ad normam can. 1216. —4) Fontem baptismalem in Sabbato Sancto benedicere." Though these functions are to be performed by the pastor or upon his authorization, this does not imply that they absolutely are prohibited in a public oratory, as

---

[70] Cf. above, Chapter 5, Article 3 and Chapter VI, Article 2.

[71] "SS. Eucharistiam publice ad infirmos in propria paroecia deferre; SS. Eucharistiam publice aut privatim tanquam Viaticum ad infirmos deferre atque in periculo mortis constitutos extrema unctione roborare; domibus benedicere Sabbato Sancto; publicam processionem extra ecclesiam ducere, benedictiones extra ecclesiam cum pompa et sollemnitate impertiri."

at least some of them may be celebrated there by the pastor or by another priest commissioned by him. This canon determines only the proper minister for these functions, the proper place is determined by other canons.

Canon 773 states that the proper place for administering solemn Baptism is the baptistery in a church or public oratory; canon 774, that every parish church must have a baptismal font, and that the local Ordinary for the convenience of the faithful may permit or command the erection of a font also in other churches or public oratories. Hence in a public oratory legitimately possessing a font, the pastor or priest commissioned by him may administer solemn Baptism and also bless the font on Holy Saturday. Sacred Ordinations and the banns of Matrimony are to be proclaimed in the parish church (can. 998 and 1023 sq.). However, if on the occasion of a special feast divine services for the parish would be held in a public oratory, it would seem that the banns could be proclaimed there, at least with the permission of the local Ordinary. The Marriage of Catholics should be celebrated in the parish church but may be celebrated in a public (or semi-public) oratory with the permission of the local Ordinary or pastor. In oratories of seminaries or of Religious women the Ordinary shall not permit it except in case of urgent necessity and after due precautions have been taken (can. 1109).

Funeral services are to be held in the parish church (can. 1216). Exceptions to this general rule in as far as they effect oratories are the following: 1) Professed Religious and their Novices are to be buried from the oratory (or church) of their Religious house or at least of their Religious institute [72] (can. 1221, § 1); but in the case of Sisters who have not been exempt from the jurisdiction of the pastor, the funeral services are to be held in the parish church (can. 1230, § 5). The first exception holds if the Religious died in or outside their Reli-

72 Unless the distance is too great and the Religious Superiors do not wish to undergo the expense of transferring the corpse (can. 1221, §2).

gious house.[73] 2) Persons resident in a seminary [74] are to be buried from the seminary oratory (church) provided they died in the seminary and did not choose another church (can. 1222 and 1368). 3) The right of choosing one's funeral church conceded by canon 1223 can be exercised in favor of an oratory only if it is expressly endowed with the "ius funerandi." Augustine [75] maintains that as the funeral service is an ecclesiastical function, it may be held in any public oratory in virtue of canon 1191, § 2, provided the deceased chose it. This view is clearly in opposition to canon 1225 [76] which is specific, and, therefore, limits canon 1191 which is general, for "Generi per speciem derogatur." [77] The only oratories that may be chosen for the funeral service are those expressly endowed with this right by the Holy See or the local Ordinary.

A very noteworthy change effected by the Code (can. 462) in its enumeration of strictly parochial rights is the administration of the Easter Communion which had been reserved to pastors for centuries.[78] Concerning

---

[73] There is, however, a controversy concerning the place for the funeral services of Religious women exempt from the pastor's jurisdiction who died outside their convent. The controversy is based on the words "generalia canonum praescripta" of can. 1230, § 5, which may refer to the general norms for the funerals of the ordinary faithful or to those for the funerals of Religious, i. e., to can. 1216 or to can. 1221. Fanfani (*De Iure Religiosorum*, n. 422) and Bouuaert-Simenon (*Manuale*, n. 805) claim that these Religious are to be buried from the parish church, or according to can. 1216. A Coronata (*De Locis et Temp. Sacris*, n. 177), whose view is substantiated by good arguments, declares that they are to be buried from their Religious church or oratory, or according to can. 1221. Vermeersch-Creusen (*Epitome*, II, n. 530, 7° and 537, 7°) defend the latter view.

[74] Vermeersch-Creusen (*Epitome*, II, n. 531) include not only the seminarians, professors, domestics, etc., but also those who were at the seminary only for a few days, e. g., parents visiting their sons. There is justification for this interpretation in the very wording of the canons: "Qui in seminario moriuntur," "Pro omnibus qui in seminario sunt."

[75] *Commentary*, VI, 129.

[76] This canon enumerates the only places which may be chosen for the funeral service. As it does not concede this right, for example, to a church of Religious in simple vows, it certainly does not imply that it does grant it to their public oratory.

[77] R. J. 34 in VI.

[78] Cf. above, Chapter V, Article 3, Section 3 and Chapter VI, Article 2, Section 2.

the Easter Communion canon 859, § 3 states: "Suadendum fidelibus ut huic praecepto satisfaciant in sua quisque paroecia; et qui in aliena paroecia satisfecerint, curent proprium parochum de adimpleto praecepto certiorem facere." From this canon it is evident that: 1) The faithful can fulfil their Easter duty anywhere, certainly, therefore, in an oratory. 2) All who have the care of souls are obliged to exhort the faithful to do so in their own parish;[79] the faithful, however, are not commanded to carry out this exhortation. 3) The concluding words of the canon—"curent proprium parochum etc."—do not imply more than a slight obligation and perhaps only a counsel for the faithful.[80] For the members of a large parish there certainly is no obligation whatever, as the pastor will not know even all of those who fulfilled their Easter duty in his own church because of their great number, the fact that his assistants also distribute Holy Communion, etc.

In addition to not infringing upon strictly parochial rights, the divine services conducted in a public oratory must be held in such a manner as not to be prejudicial to the parochial ministry. This is expressly stated in canon 482. This canon adds that if it is doubtful whether or not the parochial ministry is injured, the local Ordinary is to decide the case and to prescribe means that the injury be avoided.[81] Canon 1171 declares that the local Ordinary for a just cause may define especially the time for holding the divine services unless there is question of a church (public oratory) of exempt Religious; and even their services according to canon 609, § 3, are not to interfere with the catechetical instructions and explanation of the Gospel given in the parish church. In cases of doubt the local Ordinary is to give the decision.

---

79 Note that the Code uses the phrase "in paroecia," which is far more extensive than "in ecclesia paroeciali."

80 Cf. Cappello, *De Sacramentis,* I, n. 475. Vermeersch-Creusen, *Epitome,* II, n. 128.

81 Both regulations are repeated in can. 716 with special reference to the churches (public oratories) of confraternities and pious unions.

The will of the legislator and the wish and spirit of the Church are evident in these canons. On the success of the parochial ministry the spiritual welfare of the faithful is very greatly dependant. Anything that seriously impedes or injures that ministry is a detriment to the spiritual welfare of the faithful; but "Salus animarum est suprema lex."[82] Hence, the rights of oratories, rights though they be, cannot be exercised in such a way as to jeopardize the success of the parochial ministry; if they are so exercised, the local Ordinary can and must take means to remove the danger.

Cases are by no means rare in which the parochial ministry is positively and seriously injured by a neighboring public oratory which a large number of parishioners habitually attend. Only a few of the evil results of such attendance need be indicated. In the parish church the sermons and instructions are (presumed to be) given with special reference to the needs of the parishioners; here alone are the parish announcements made, the banns of Matrimony proclaimed, etc. In the oratory, even if there is a sermon, it is not specially adapted to the needs of the parishioners, and information concerning parish affairs, which they should have, is not given them. Another evil, by no means negligible, is the decrease in the parish revenue. In most of the parishes of our country one of the principal sources of the income absolutely necessary for the maintenance of the parish, and, therefore, of the parochial ministry, is the Sunday collection. That this collection is notably diminished by the habitual attendance of a large number of parishioners at a neighboring oratory is too evident to require any proof. In some instances, owing to local conditions, the very existence of the parish may be at stake. What means may the local Ordinary use to protect the parish?

Canon 467, § 2 declares: "Monendi sunt fideles ut frequenter, ubi commode id fieri possit, ad suas paroeciales

---

[82] Cf. S. C. Consist., decr. "*Maxima cura,*" Aug. 20, 1910; *Acta Apostolicae Sedis,* II (1910), 636.

ecclesias accedant ibique divinis officiis intersint et verbum Dei audiant." But this canon does not impose a strict obligation on the faithful as is evident from its wording, and a mere exhortation may be entirely ineffective. Canon 1171 gives the local Ordinary the right to define *especially* (*praesertim*) the time at which the divine services are to be held in a public oratory (a non-parochial church). But this remedy may be equally ineffective, as the parishioners, nevertheless, may neglect the parish church and frequent the oratory. The insertion of the word "praesertim" in this canon is noteworthy, as it clearly implies that there are other means which the Ordinary may use to attain the end desired. Canon 483 states that the local Ordinary may command that catechetical instructions and an explanation of the Gospel be given and feast and fast days announced in a church (public oratory), if, in his judgment, it is situated at such distance from the parish church that the neighboring parishioners cannot go to the parish church without grave inconvenience. But this canon is concerned only with churches (public oratories) that are at a considerable distance from the parish church. Canon 1345 states that a brief explanation of the Gospel or of some part of Christian doctrine should be given in all churches and public oratories on feast days of precept at the Masses which the faithful attend, and that if the bishop issues a ruling to this effect, it must be obeyed by all the clergy even though they be exempt Religious. The observance of this canon may eliminate one of the evil results indicated above; the others, especially the decrease in the revenue, might be combated in other ways—but perhaps not successfully. Often the defection of a large number of parishioners is due to the pastor; the appointment of a new one may induce them again to frequent their own parish church.

If, despite the use of the above and similar remedies, the detriment to the parish continues or even increases, can the bishop adopt more stringent means, and in particular: 1) Can he prohibit or limit the number of certain sacred functions, e.g., High Masses? 2) Can he forbid the parishioners to frequent the oratory on Sundays,[83] or what would be the equivalent, can he command the responsible persons not to admit them? There are serious reasons for questioning the right of the Ordinary to either power.

By canon 1191, § 2, all sacred functions may be celebrated in a dedicated public oratory "salvo contrario rubricarum praescripto." By canon 1193, all sacred functions may be celebrated in a semi-public oratory "nisi obstent rubricae *aut Ordinarius aliqua exceperit.*" The silence of canon 1191 concerning the right of the Ordinary to forbid certain functions in a public oratory seems to be more than a merely negative silence; it seems to be a positive denial of this power.[84] Moreover, the primary purpose of a public oratory is the convenience or benefit of a corporation or of certain private individuals. If the Ordinary forbids certain sacred functions, and in as far as he does forbid them, in so far does the oratory fail to attain its primary purpose. It is true that this may be said also of a semi-public oratory which is intended for the convenience of a community or of a group of faithful; but for a semi-public oratory the Code expressly states that the Ordinary may impose limitations, a right that seems denied him in the case of a public oratory.

In favor of the right of the Ordinary, an argument may be deduced from canon 482, which states: "Ecclesiae rector potest divina officia etiam sollemnia ibidem celebrare .... *dummodo non noceant ministerio paroeciali,*" and, according to canon 1191, § 1, this norm must be applied also to public oratories. This canon apparently demands as a "conditio sine qua non" that the services do not injure the parochial ministry. Hence, if all other

---

83 Their attendance on ordinary week days is not in question, as that usually does not injure the parochial ministry.

84 Hence, though the use of "praesertim" in can. 1171 clearly implies the right of the Ordinary to use other means besides determining the hour of all or certain sacred functions, it does not seem to include the right of prohibiting these functions.

means fail to prevent this injury, it would seem that this canon gives the Ordinary the necessary power to prohibit certain functions provided the prohibition prevents the injury. But, unless he forbade all services (not only, e.g., High Masses, but also Low Masses), the parishioners, nevertheless, might continue to neglect their parish church and go to the oratory for the functions that were still permitted and thus his purpose would not be attained. An Ordinary scarcely would forbid all functions even if it were certain that he had the power to do so; such a measure would be too radical, as the oratory would cease to serve the purpose for which it was erected and dedicated. Moreover, certain persons by law [85] or by a papal indult have the right to a public oratory, the advantages of which no local Ordinary may deprive them. In virtue of these juridical and practical objections it appears that the local Ordinary cannot forbid all or certain sacred functions in a public oratory.

The reason for questioning the right of the local Ordinary to forbid the parishioners to attend the services in a public oratory is to be found in the Code's definition of a public oratory. Canon 1188, which gives this definition, declares that all the faithful have the right [86] to be present in a public oratory at least at the time of divine services. It is especially this right of the faithful that distinguishes a public from a semi-public oratory. The corporation or private individuals for whose convenience the public oratory was primarily erected certainly cannot restrict this right of the faithful. May the bishop do so? On this question Woywod writes: "By the law of the Code the people have a right to enter public oratories at the time of divine services, and that right seems to be one of the essential features of a public oratory; wherefore, it does not seem possible to allow the erection of a public oratory and then deprive it of

85 E. g., clerical Religious by can. 497, § 2.

86 The Code indeed states that this right must be legitimately established. Can this clause perhaps be interpreted in such a manner that it gives the Ordinary the power to limit or recall this right? No commentator that has been consulted offers such an interpretation.

one of its essential rights."[87] Moreover, the argument may be advanced that as the faithful have a right to be present in a public oratory they have this right not only against the possessors of the oratory, but also against the local Ordinary, for "Ubi lex non distinguit, nec nos distinguere debemus"; hence only the legislator who conceded the right can recall it. In commenting on this right of the faithful, Vermeersch-Creusen, with a brevity that is misleading, write: "Ius tamen istud populi esse non debet respectu auctoritatis ecclesiasticae; huic enim integrum est etiam ecclesiam claudere populo."[88] The bishop can indeed close a church or public oratory by reducing it to profane use provided it no longer can be used for divine worship (can. 1187), and also by an interdict which, however, can be inflicted only for a grave crime[89] (can. 2242 and 2269). But, beyond these two possibilities, his power is not so evident as to justify so apodictic and sweeping an assertion; for a public oratory, as well as a church, is dedicated "*perpetuo* ad *publicum* Dei cultum" (can. 1191, § 2).

But despite these and other arguments it is not improbable that the Ordinary may have the power to issue such a prohibition. The letter and the spirit of the Code clearly demand the protection of the parochial ministry. If serious detriment to that ministry cannot be obviated in any other way, then it would seem that he may be justified in protecting it by forbidding the parishioners to frequent the oratory at certain times. In last analysis, this is the only direct remedy and may be the only effective one; and even if used, the primary purpose of the public oratory—the convenience of those for whom it was erected—still can be attained. The right of the faithful is indeed limited thereby, but it is not destroyed, for they still could frequent the oratory at all times when their doing so would not injure their own church. More-

---

87 *The Homiletic and Pastoral Review,* XXVI (1925), 168.

88 *Epitome,* II, n. 498.

89 In the case under discussion there is no crime nor is there question of reducing the oratory to profane use.

over, even as a mere limitation of their right, the prohibition would be only temporary.[90] As soon as the faithful again become accustomed to go to their own church, the prohibition would be recalled, and it is not likely that they soon would frequent the oratory in such numbers as to cause the recurrence of the injury.

Taking all arguments into consideration, the law on the question seems doubtful. In a practical case if the bishop would forbid the parishioners to frequent the oratory at certain times (or if he would command the responsible parties to refuse them admission), he would have to be obeyed;[91] meanwhile recourse could be had to the Holy See by the persons interested. But one more remark need be added. If despite the prohibition of the bishop the parishioners would attend Sunday Mass in the oratory, they would thereby fulfil the obligation of a preceptive Mass; for the prohibition of the bishop cannot be made or interpreted contrary to canon 1249 which clearly states that the law of attending Mass can be satisfied in any public oratory.

Finally, canon 1191, § 2 states that in a public oratory all sacred functions may be celebrated "*salvo contrario rubricarum praescripto.*" The principal limitations imposed on oratories by the laws of liturgy have reference to the last three days of Holy Week and thus may be summarized:[92] The sacred functions of these days are permitted only in those oratories in which the Blessed Sacrament is reserved. When held in an oratory, these functions must be celebrated solemnly (i. e., with deacon and sub-deacon) according to the rites prescribed in the Roman Missal. The simple rites of the "Memoriale Ri-

---

90 If it would be perpetual, it would make the public oratory a semi-public one, which at least in the case of oratories conceded by the Holy See, either in the Code or by particular indult, is clearly beyond his competency.

91 "In re communi potior est conditio prohibentis;" R. J. 56 in VI.

92 Cf. S. R. C., June 14, 1659; Aug. 31, 1839; March 16, 1876; May 9, 1884; Dec. 9, 1899; D. A., 1120, 2799, 3390, 3608, 4049. Cf. also Callewaert, *Caeremoniale*, n. 423 sq.; Van der Stappen, *Sacra Liturgia*, III, Q. 157-160; Many, *De Missa*, n. 14 sq.

tuum" of Benedict XIII[93] cannot be used in oratories[94] unless this privilege has been obtained from the Holy See.[95] The sacred functions of these three days are obligatory in no oratory; if, however, the functions of Maundy Thursday are held, those of Good Friday (which are a continuation of those of the preceding day) must be celebrated. If the functions of these three days are not celebrated, one Mass, nevertheless, may be offered and also Holy Communion distributed on Maundy Thursday in the oratories of Regulars.[96] The other prescriptions of liturgy as also the liturgical laws contained in the Code (especially in can. 801-869 and 1265-1275) must be observed in oratories as well as in churches. Of these laws only the following need be mentioned here:

1) All priests[97] (Secular or Religious) wishing to offer Mass in a public oratory must offer the Mass prescribed by the calendar of the oratory even though the Mass be proper to Religious. Particular rites, however, that may be proper to Religious Orders (e. g., the Dominican Rite) are not to be adopted.[98] 2) On Christmas night in all Religious or Pious houses having an oratory with the

---

93 The "Memoriale Rituum" was revised in 1920 under Benedict XV.

94 Only in parish churches in which there are not sufficient clergy or vestments may the "Memoriale Rituum" be used without special permission.

95 The latest quinquennial faculties (V, Facultates S. R. C., n. 10; cf. Vermeersch-Creusen, *Epitome,* II, n. 871, Appendix) give our bishops the power of conceding the use of the "Memoriale Rituum" to non-parochial churches and to public and semi-public oratories.

96 This double privilege, however, is restricted to oratories of Regulars strictly so-called as was stated expressly by the S. R. C., Dec. 9, 1899 (D. A., 4049). Hence the view of Augustine (*Commentary,* IV, 161) extending it to seminaries and pious communities (for which the above decree clearly states an Apostolic indult is required) must be rejected, as the only authority he offers is an earlier decree of the same Congregation (June 28, 1821;D. A., 2616) which is concerned only with parish churches. The new quinquennial faculties (IV, Facultates S. C. Relig., n. 7; cf. Vermeersch-Creusen, *Epitome,* II, n. 871, Appendix) give our bishops the power to grant this double privilege to any Religious community.

97 Cardinals and bishops enjoy the privilege of offering holy Mass according to their own calendar in all churches and oratories (can. 239, §1, 9° and 349, §1, 1°).

98 *Missale Romanum, Additiones et Variationes in Rubricis Missalis,* Tit. 4, n. 6. The same regulation is to be observed whenever a priest of one rite offers Mass in the public oratory of another rite; cf. can. 816-819.

faculty of habitually reserving the Blessed Sacrament, one priest may offer three Masses;[99] all who attend fulfil the obligation of hearing Mass, and Holy Communion may be administered to those who desire to receive It (can. 821, § 3). 3) With the permission of the local Ordinary the Blessed Sacrament may be reserved in the principal oratory (public or semi-public) of Religious houses, of Pious institutes and of ecclesiastical colleges ruled by clerics or Religious. For all other oratories an Apostolic indult is required, though in a public oratory the local Ordinary for a just cause may permit the Blessed Sacrament to be retained temporarily (can. 1265). 4) In any oratory in which the Blessed Sacrament is reserved, private exposition (with the ciborium) may be held for any just cause, the permission of the Ordinary not being required. Public exposition (with the ostensorium) may be held in public oratories[100] in which the Blessed Sacrament is reserved[101] at the Masses and Vespers of the Feast of Corpus Christi and during its Octave; at other times only "ex justa et gravi causa praesertim publica et de Ordinarii loci licentia" (can. 1274). The public exposition of the Forty Hours is obligatory for all public oratories in which the Blessed Sacrament is reserved (can. 1275). Benediction with the Blessed Sacrament is prescribed at every public exposition and is permitted at every private exposition.[102] Many oratories, however, enjoy far more extensive privileges which were obtained by particular concession or through legitimate

---

99 The "Prima Missa in nocte" is not to be offered three times, but the three Masses are to be offered successively as they are given in the Missal. If the priest offers only one Mass on Christmas night (as the canon permits him to do), he must observe the time prescribed by the rubrics for the other two Masses.

100 Cappello (*De Sacramentis*, I, n. 417) restricts this right to churches as the mere wording of can. 1274 seems to do; but Blat (*Commentarium*, IV, n. 142), Bouuaert-Simenon (*Manuale*, n. 841), Cocchi (*Commentarium*, V, n. 104) and most other authors extend it also to public oratories in virtue of can. 1191, § 1.

101 Cf. *Pont. Comm. ad C. I. C. auth. interpret.*, July 14, 1922; *Acta Apostolicae Sedis*, XIV (1922) 529.

102 S. R. C., July 12, 1889, and Nov. 30, 1895; D. A., 3713 and 3875.

custom.[103] As only a few of these privileges are revoked by the Code,[104] all others may still be used (can. 4, 5, 27 and 30).

As the principal exceptions and limitations to the sacred functions that may be celebrated in public oratories have been given, it is not necessary to offer a detailed enumeration of those that are permitted. The general statement, therefore, will suffice to conclude this section that all sacred functions that are not forbidden by the laws indicated above may be celebrated in any public oratory.

Article 5: Miscellanea.

The rector of a public oratory is appointed by the local Ordinary or at least must be approved by him if others have a lawfully established right of nomination, presentation or election. Even if the public oratory pertains to exempt Religious whose major Superior has the right of naming its rector, the approbation of the local Ordinary is necessary. If the oratory is annexed to a seminary or college governed by clerics, the rector thereof is also the rector of the public oratory unless other provisions have been made (can. 480, 698 and 1191, § 1). In all cases the local Ordinary can remove the rector for any just cause; if he is a Religious he is removable at the will of his Religious Superior and of the local Ordinary, neither requiring the other's consent, though each must notify the other of the removal (can. 486 and 454, § 5).

The rector has charge of the celebration of all sacred functions. Without his (at least presumed) permission or that of some other legitimate Superior, no one may celebrate holy Mass or any other sacred function in the oratory (can. 482 and 484).

Unless other provisions have been made by legitimate

---

103 Cf. *Concilii Plenarii Baltimorensis II Acta et Decreta*, n. 375.

104 Can. 1267 revokes all privileges of reserving the Blessed Sacrament within the choir or cloister of nuns and within Religious or Pious institutes but outside their principal church or oratory. Cf. *Pont. Comm. ad C. I. C. auth interpret.*, June 2, 1918; *Acta Apostolicae Sedis*, X (1918), 346.

custom, convention or the local Ordinary, the administration of the goods destined for the repair and embellishment of the oratory and for the celebration of divine services is entrusted to the rector (can. 485 and 1182). But even if a board of trustees has charge of this administration, it dare not interfere with the spiritual administration of the oratory which pertains exclusively to the rector under the supervision of the local Ordinary (can. 1184 and 1261). In the administration of the temporalities of an oratory the general norms (can. 1518-1528) for the administration of church property must be observed. The funds required for the maintenance of the oratory and of divine services are to be supplied by those for whose convenience the oratory was erected. Oblations freely made by the faithful who visit the oratory are to be employed for these purposes; but no admission fee may be exacted from them, as admission to divine services must be entirely free, every custom to the contrary being reprobated by the Code (can. 1181, 1182, 1186, 1297).[105]

Though not preceptive, it is becoming that a public oratory have bells by which the faithful may be invited to the divine services. These bells must be consecrated or blessed according to the rites of the approved liturgical books,[106] the ministers for these functions being the same as for the consecration or blessing of the oratory itself. The use of these bells is regulated exclusively by the ecclesiastical authorities; they are not to be used for merely profane purposes except in case of necessity, in virtue of a legitimate custom, by the permission of the Ordinary or in accordance with the stipulations made by the donor and sanctioned by the Ordinary (can. 1169). The number of bells is not limited by the Code,[107] but

---

105 Cf. also *Concilii Plenarii Baltimorensis II Acta et Decreta*, n. 396; *Concilii Plenarii Baltimorensis III Acta et Decreta*, n. 288.

106 The Pontifical (Pars II, *De Benedictione Signi vel Campanae*) if the bells are to be consecrated, the Ritual (*Benedictio Campanae quae ad usum ecclesiae benedictae vel oratorii inserviat*) if they are to be blessed.

107 According to the old law (c. 1, *de officio custodis*, I, 5, in Extravag. com.) only one bell was permitted in the churches or oratories of Mendicant Religious.

may be by particular legislation; no particular law, however, may prohibit all bells in a public oratory as such a prohibition would be contrary to the above canon. The ringing of bells is prohibited during the last three days of Holy Week by the laws of liturgy and during a general local interdict by canon 2271; but even during the interdict they may be rung on the Feasts of Christmas, Easter, Pentecost, Corpus Christi and the Assumption of the Blessed Virgin (can. 2270).

A public oratory that has been dedicated is a sacred place and as such is exempt from civil jurisdiction and is subject to that of the legitimate ecclesiastical authorities (can. 1160). It, likewise, enjoys the right of asylum in virtue of which fugitives seeking refuge therein may not be removed, except in case of urgent necessity, without the consent of the Ordinary or at least of its rector (can. 1179). The exemption from civil jurisdiction is proper to all sacred places, the right of asylum only to dedicated churches and public oratories. Although the civil codes of most modern nations recognize neither prerogative, they are not thereby destroyed even though their practical application is rendered difficult and often impossible. The Church as a perfect and independent society is justified in claiming both rights for her sacred places. If she has greatly modified the right of asylum,[108] it is only because it is not as necessary as formerly when it so often proved instrumental in averting rank injustice by securing for the fugitive the benefit of a fair trial.

Finally, as is becoming to the house of God, a public oratory shall be kept neat and clean; business transactions and fairs even if held for a pious purpose, and in general, everything that is not in harmony with the sa-

---

108 Formerly only the bishop could give permission to extradite a fugitive; by the Code also the rector of the church or public oratory is empowered to do so and in urgent cases no permission is required. Moreover, the penalties of the old law (cf. e. g., Pius IX, const. "*Apostolicae Sedis,*" Oct. 12, 1869, § 2, n. 5; Fontes, 552) against the violators of this right are abrogated by the Code (can. 6, 5°).

cred character of the oratory must be excluded (can. 1178). Even rooms directly above or beneath the oratory shall not be used for merely profane purposes (can. 1164, § 2). The zeal of the Church for her places of worship has been evident throughout the centuries. Splendor and magnificence she occasionally has commended, but cleanliness and neatness she always has demanded.[109] By consecration or blessing the oratory is dedicated to God's service and should be used for His service alone: "Semel Deo dedicatum non est ad usus humanos ulterius transferendum."[110] Even without an ecclesiastical law, the natural reverence due to sacred places which are the scenes of the most solemn and august acts of religion, ought to secure alike their cleanliness and their exclusively sacred use. The maintenance of both is the privilege as well as the duty of the rector and of those for whose convenience the oratory was erected; it is also among the things which the local Ordinary is to investigate on the occasion of his quinquennial visitation (can. 344).[111]

---

109 Cf. Benedict XIV, ep. encycl. "*Annus qui,*" Feb. 19, 1749, § 1; Fontes, 395.

110 R. J. 51 in VI.

111 All public oratories are subject to this visitation of the local Ordinary except those of Religious Orders (can. 512).

CHAPTER IX.

The Laws Governing Semi-Public Oratories.

The Code law on semi-public oratories is concerned with: 1) their erection; 2) their dedication; 3) the celebration of divine services; 4) their exclusively sacred use; 5) their lawful reduction to profane use. In this sequence these topics will be investigated. In considering the rights and privileges of semi-public oratories the ruling of canon 1189 must be remembered which ascribes both to the private oratories of cardinals and of (residential or titular) bishops. This chapter on semi-public oratories will be comparatively brief, for many of the subjects examined in the rather lengthy treatise on public oratories will be applied to semi-public oratories by a mere reference; moreover, the Code itself affords only a few canons expressly devoted to semi-public oratories.

Oratoria semi-publica erigi nequeunt sine Ordinarii licentia (can. 1192, § 1).

The Code here demands the permission of the Ordinary for the erection of a semi-public oratory. All the persons mentioned as Ordinaries in canon 198, § 1 are competent to grant this permission, for the Code uses the term "Ordinarius," not "Ordinarius loci;" hence also the major Superiors of exempt clerical Religious are empowered to give this permission. The power of these Religious Superiors, however, is restricted: 1) To semi-public oratories strictly so-called which alone are under consideration here;[1] 2) To those erected for and in connection with their Religious houses, as outside their

1 To erect a public oratory (to which they have a right by can. 497, § 2) in a definite and specified place they require the written permission of the local Ordinary as was stated in the last chapter, while for the erection of a private oratory their powers are very limited, as will be shown in the next chapter.

Religious houses they have no jurisdiction in this matter.[2] Consequently, if they desire to have a (semi-public) cemetery chapel, the permission of the local Ordinary is necessary for its erection.[3]

The limitation placed upon the power of the Vicar General by canon 1162, § 1, in consequence of which he requires a special mandate to permit the erection of a public oratory or church, is not repeated in the law for the erection of a semi-public oratory. Hence by his ordinary power he may give permission to erect a semi-public oratory unless the bishop reserved this right to himself as he may do in virtue of canon 368, § 1. But even if the bishop did not reserve this right, the Vicar General cannot lawfully exercise it contrary to the will of the bishop (can. 369, § 2), and if in a particular case the bishop has refused permission to allow the erection of a semi-public oratory, the Vicar General cannot validly permit it without the explicit consent of the bishop (can. 44, § 2). As the other Ordinaries mentioned in canon 198 are local Ordinaries in their own name, their power of permitting the erection of these oratories is limited only by the boundaries of the territory over which they exercise jurisdiction.

The Code does not demand that this permission of the Ordinary be given in writing as it does when there is question of a public oratory or church (can. 1162, § 1 and 1192, § 1); nevertheless, it is expedient that written permission be given also for a semi-public oratory, as such documentary proof will be very desirable if the right of the community to the oratory ever is contested. The concession or refusal of permission to erect a semi-public oratory is left entirely to the judgment of the Ordinary

2 This limitation of their power was emphasized already in c. 14, X, *de privilegiis, V*, 33, and in *c.* 4, *de privilegiis*, V, 7, in VI; cf. also S. R. C., Nov. 10, 1906; D. A., 4190.

3 Cf. A Coronata, *De Locis et Temp. Sacris*, n. 85, d.

who, however, must observe the following laws:

Ordinarius hanc licentiam ne concedat, nisi prius per se vel per alium ecclesiasticum virum oratorium visitaverit et decenter instructum repererit (can. 1192, § 2).

It is evident that reference is made here to the canonical rather than to the material erection of the oratory, for there is question of visiting and inspecting the oratory to discover whether it will be a suitable place for the celebration of the sacred functions, especially of the holy Sacrifice of the Mass. If the Ordinary does not make this inspection personally, he must select as his delegate an ecclesiastic, that is, a person who is in the clerical state. The investigation must comprise the building or room that is destined to be the oratory, the sacred vessels, utensils and vestments to be used in the sacred functions, the pictures and statues erected in the oratory, etc. If the oratory with its equipment is found to satisfy the requirements of the laws of liturgy and of the Code, final permission for its use for the sacred functions is then given.

In collegiis aut convictibus iuventuti instituendae, in gymnasiis, lyceis, arcibus, praesidiis militum, carceribus, xenodochiis, etc., praeter oratorium principale, alia minora ne erigantur, nisi, Ordinarii iudicio, necessitas aut magna utilitas id exigat (can. 1192, § 4).

This law clearly indicates that it is the wish of the Church that as a rule the Ordinary shall allow only one oratory in these institutions. But as the purpose of a semi-public oratory is the convenience of the community for whom it is erected, the Code permits the Ordinary to allow a plurality of oratories if that purpose cannot be attained by one oratory. The sole judge of the necessity or great utility of additional oratories is the Ordinary; in this the Code is far more liberal than the decree of the Congregation of Rites of March 8, 1879,[4] which demanded a special faculty from the Holy See for permitting the

---

[4] § 2; D. A., 3484.

erection of a secondary oratory. As a plurality of oratories in Religious houses is not referred to in this canon, the Ordinary (the major Superior for exempt clerical Religious) may allow additional oratories in these houses more readily than in the institutions mentioned in this canon. Although the Code calls these additional oratories "minora oratoria" and some authors refer to them as private oratories, nevertheless they are semi-public as is evident from the definitions of canon 1188.

The Code law on the erection of semi-public oratories, therefore, is very simple and can be summarized in one sentence; their erection is determined ultimately by the will and judgment of the Ordinary.

§ 1. Oratoria domestica nec consecrari nec benedici possunt more ecclesiarum.

§ 2. Licet oratoria domestica et semi-publica communi locorum domorumve benedictione aut nulla benedictione donentur . . . (can. 1196).

Comparing this canon with canons 1191 and 1165, the following conclusions are evident: 1) Although a public oratory must be dedicated, the same obligation is not to be extended to a semi-public oratory; 2) Although a private oratory cannot be consecrated or solemnly blessed, either sacred rite may be applied to a semi-public oratory. Therefore, unlike either of the other species of oratories there is neither an obligation nor a prohibition to dedicate a semi-public oratory. This is so simple and clear that any comment would be superfluous. If not dedicated, a semi-public oratory may be blessed with the ordinary "Benedictio Loci vel Domus," [5] but even this merely invocative blessing is not prescribed. If a semi-public oratory is to be dedicated, all the regulations must be observed which were given in the last chapter concerning the rite and minister of dedication, the celebration of the titular feast and of the anniversary of consecration, the violation and the reconciliation of

---

5 *Rituale Romanum,* Tit. 8, c. 6.

a dedicated place, the loss of consecration or blessing, etc. Dedicated semi-public oratories as sacred places are entitled to the exemption from civil jurisdiction referred to in canon 1160, but do not enjoy the right of asylum of canon 1179.

In oratoriis semi-publicis, legitime erectis, omnia divina officia functionesve ecclessiasticae celebrari possunt, nisi obstent rubricae aut Ordinarius aliqua exceperit (can. 1193).

This canon allows the celebration of all sacred functions in a semi-public oratory that has been legitimately erected except such as the rubrics or the Ordinary exclude. Hence the exceptions and limitations mentioned in the last chapter which have reference to the parochial rights, the functions of Holy Week, and to the reservation, exposition and benediction of the Blessed Sacrament must be applied also to semi-public oratories. In the celebration of holy Mass all priests (Secular or Religious) must follow the calendar of the semi-public oratory [6] unless the Mass is celebrated in one of the secondary oratories (referred to above in can. 1192, § 4), in which case the celebrant is to follow his own calendar.[7]

The Ordinary having the right to exclude or limit the celebration of certain functions in a semi-public oratory is the major Superior of exempt clerical Religious in reference to their own oratories, the local Ordinary for all other oratories. In institutions that have several oratories, restrictions very frequently are imposed on the

---

6 This will be the diocesan calendar unless the oratory possesses its own proper calendar. All Religious Orders and many Religious Congregations have their own proper calendar. Tertiary Congregations aggregated to a First Order have the calendar of the Order to which they are aggregated. Cf. S. R. C., Feb. 28, 1914; *Acta Apostolicae Sedis,* VI (1914), 118.

7 *Missale Romanum, Additiones et Variationes in Rubricis Missalis,* Tit. 4, n. 6. Cf. Brehm, *Synopsis,* p. 211 sq. However, Battistini (*Eph. Liturg.,* XXXV [1921], 225 and XL [1926], 177) defends the view as probable which maintains that in these secondary oratories "sacerdotes extranei" have the option of following either their own calendar or that of the oratory in which they celebrate.

secondary oratories [8] which as a rule are intended only for the celebration of holy Mass. There usually is more justification for limiting the sacred functions in oratories of the laity than in those of Religious, and in the oratories of small communities than in those of large communities. Although the number, nature and extent of the restrictions are left to the judgment of the Ordinary, he cannot impose any that are contrary to the prescriptions of the Code; thus, for example, though he can forbid the faithful to frequent a semi-public oratory, he cannot declare that the obligation of a preceptive Mass cannot be satisfied by those who nevertheless attend Mass in that semi-public oratory, for canon 1249 clearly states that this obligation can be satisfied in any semi-public oratory. But if the restrictions do not contravene the law of the Code, the Ordinary may impose them not only at the time of the erection of the oratory, but also afterwards; they should not, however, be so general or so numerous as to frustrate the purpose of the oratory which is the convenience of those for whom it was erected.

Safeguarding, therefore, the laws of liturgy and of the Code, the rights of pastors and the prescriptions of the Ordinary, all sacred functions may be celebrated in a semi-public oratory.

Licet oratoria domestica et semi-publica communi locorum domorumve benedictione aut nulla benedictione donentur, debent tamen esse divino tantum cultui reservata et ab omnibus domesticis usibus libera (can. 1196, § 2).

Even though it is true that an oratory that has not been consecrated or blessed with the constitutive blessing of the Ritual is not a sacred place in the canonical acceptation of that term (can. 1154), nevertheless, it possesses a sacred character received from the celebration of the holy Sacrifice on its altars. For this reason

8 The Code itself does so in can. 1265 and 1267; cf. also the liturgical limitations imposed by the S. R. C., Nov. 10, 1906; D. A., 4192.

its exclusively sacred use is prescribed by the above canon. This is in harmony with the decree of the Consistorial Congregation in 1912[9] and with the constant legislation of the Church that all places in which the Divine Mysteries are celebrated shall not be used for other purposes. Although canon 1164, § 2—which forbids the use of rooms directly above or under a church (public oratory) for merely profane purposes—is not extended to semi-public oratories, still the Holy See frequently has forbidden that the rooms directly and immediately above these oratories be used as dormitories or bedrooms, tolerating such use only in case of necessity and then demanding that a "baldacchino" be placed above the altar in which the Blessed Sacrament is reserved.[10]

Oratorium (semi-publicum) ad usus profanos converti nequit sine eiusdem Ordinarii auctoritate (can. 1192, § 3).

The Ordinary whose permission is here required to reduce the oratory to profane use is the one who permitted its erection, that is, the major Superior of exempt clerical Religious for their oratories, the local Ordinary for all other oratories. This regulation is in accordance with the old axiom of law, "Omnis res, per quascunque causas nascitur, per easdem dissolvitur,"[11] and has reference to the permanent reduction of the oratory to profane use, though it includes also its temporary use for these purposes.[12] It is evident that the Ordinary may reduce to profane use an oratory that was not dedicated far more readily than one that was dedicated; but even if it was consecrated, the authorization of the Ordinary suffices to reduce it to profane use.

---

[9] Dec. 10; cf. *Acta Apostolicae Sedis, IV* (1912), 724.

[10] Cf. S. R. C., May 11, 1641; Sept. 12, 1840; July 27, 1878; Nov. 23, 1880; D. A., 756, 2812, 3460, 3525.

[11] C. 1, X, *de regulis juris*, V, 41.

[12] Thus an Ordinary would not be exceeding the power which he has in virtue of this canon if he would allow an oratory to be used temporarily as a hospital in time of war, during a serious epidemic, etc. In case of necessity this permission of the Ordinary could be presumed.

CHAPTER X.

The Laws Governing Private Oratories.

In the examination of the pre-Code law it was shown that from the first centuries of the Christian era to the Council of Trent the permission of the bishop was required for the celebration of Mass in private oratories, but that the Council of Trent demanded the permission of the Holy See. The Code adopts the Tridentine law, but concedes certain limited rights to the Ordinaries. The principal laws of the Code on private oratories are contained in canons 1194-1196, the last three canons in its tract on oratories; the examination of these laws will conclude this dissertation.

In privatis coemeteriorum aediculis, de quibus in can. 1190, Ordinarius loci permittere habitualiter potest etiam plurium Missarum celebrationem; in aliis oratoriis domesticis, nonnisi unius Missae, per modum actus, in casu aliquo extraordinario, iusta et rationabili de causa; Ordinarius autem has permissiones ne elargiatur, nisi ad normam can. 1192, § 2 (can. 1194).

As was stated above,[1] there are few private cemetery chapels in our country. Very many of our cemeteries have their own chapels, but these are public, not private oratories, and, as such, are governed by the laws for public oratories. But wherever private cemetery chapels exist, the local Ordinary is empowered by the above canon to permit habitually the celebration of even several Masses. In granting him the two-fold power of permitting several Masses daily (for thus must this passage be interpreted), and of giving this permission habitually, this canon affords a two-fold exception to the general law

[1] Cf. Chapter VII, Article 2, n. 3.

of the Code for private oratories.[2] A further exception in favor of private cemetery chapels is made by canon 1249, which states that all who attend Mass therein fulfil the obligation of a preceptive Mass.[3]

These private cemetery chapels may be erected by any of the faithful,[4] but the concession of the celebration of Mass therein is reserved to the local Ordinary. In virtue of a privilege conceded in the Missal,[5] the holy Masses in private cemetery chapels may be Requiem Masses on all the days of the year[6] except Sundays and feasts of precept, even though suppressed, Doubles of the First and Second Class, even though transferred, and the Privileged Ferials, Vigils and Octaves. It is evident that canon 1202, § 2, which prohibits the burial of a corpse under an altar, and the celebration of Mass on any altar that is not at least a meter's distance from the nearest tomb, must be observed in these private cemetery chapels. Canon 1205, however, which forbids the burial of any corpse (except those of certain dignitaries) in a church or public oratory, is not to be extended to these chapels, for, according to canon 1190, they are erected by the faithful expressly for their own sepulture.

In all other (non-cemetery) private oratories the local Ordinary may permit not several but one holy Mass to be celebrated. Canon 1194 states that he can grant this permission only: 1) *Per modum actus*: Hence he cannot grant it habitually or perpetually as the bishops could do before the Council of Trent; 2) *Iusta et rationabili de causa*: Although in virtue of the wording of the Tridentine decree, "Quanta cura," the bishops seemed to

---

2 It likewise offers a complete departure from the old law (Tridentine and post-Tridentine) which reserved to the Holy See the right of granting habitual permission to offer Mass in any private oratory.

3 This right was admitted by the general decree of the S. R. C., Jan. 23, 1899 (D. A., 4007), but according to this decree these oratories were semi-public.

4 Provided they obtain the written permission demanded by can. 1209 for the erection of any special burial place in a blessed cemetery.

5 *Additiones et Variationes in Rubricis Missalis,* Tit. 3, n. 8.

6 This privilege ceases as soon as the cemetery no longer is used for the burial of the dead even though the corpses already interred there are not transferred; cf. Brehm, *Synopsis,* p. 203.

be forbidden to permit Mass in private oratories under any circumstances, canonists, nevertheless, almost unanimously interpreted that decree as not withholding from the bishops the power of permitting Mass therein "gravi de causa et per modum actus"; this interpretation was confirmed by decisions of the Congregations of the Propaganda and of the Council,[7] and is adopted in this canon which, however, demands not a grave cause but only a just and reasonable one; 3) *In casu aliquo extraordinario*: By the insertion of this phrase the Code further restricts the power of the Ordinary in as far as it declares that he cannot exercise it except in an extraordinary case; hence, the mere fact that there is a just and reasonable cause for granting the permission does not warrant its concession unless the Ordinary judges that the case in question is also an extrordinary, exceptional or urgent case.

Although it is left to the judgment of the Ordinary to decide when the above conditions are verified, the wording of the canon is sufficiently emphatic to induce him to use sparingly the power which it grants. If, however, he judges that the circumstances justify its exercise, his power is not limited to one single Mass as the phrase "celebrationem unius Missae" of the canon may seem to imply, but to one daily Mass. This daily Mass he may permit as long as the circumstances that warrant its concession continue. Thus, for example, if he granted this permission to an institution (or to a family) that was quarantined, he could permit one Mass to be offered in its private oratory every day that the quarantine was in force. Cappello [8] and Cocchi [9] imply that the Ordinary shall not concede permission for more than eight or ten days at a time, but admit that he may renew this permission as often as the reason that urged its concession still continues. The more common opinion, however, maintains that the Ordinary by one act may grant permis-

7 Cf. above, Chapter VI, Article 1.

8 *De Sacramentis,* I, n. 750.

9 *Commentarium,* V, n. 32, b.

sion for as long a time as the cause continues, thus interpreting the phrase "per modum actus" as equivalent to "durante causa." But if it is foreseen that the cause will continue for an indefinite or very great length of time, the Ordinary should refer the case to the Holy See, though meanwhile he may permit one daily Mass.[10]

That this power of the Ordinary is not limited to one single Mass is defended by almost all commentators of the Code and is in harmony with the pre-code discipline; it seems confirmed, also, by canon 822, § 4, which grants the Ordinary the faculty of conceding the privilege of a portable altar [11] under the same conditions under which canon 1194 grants him the right of permitting Mass in a private oratory, but omits that canon's phrase "unius Missae." Another very noteworthy fact is evident from canon 822, § 4: Although canon 1194 mentions only the local Ordinary as competent to permit Mass in a private oratory, canon 822, § 4 states that the major Superior of exempt Religious can (when the necessary conditions are present) concede the right of a portable altar within their Religious houses. In virtue of this faculty these Superiors must be included under canon 1194 as having the power of allowing the celebration of Mass in a private oratory within their Religious houses whenever the conditions demanded by this canon are present.

Finally, canon 1194 states that the Ordinary shall not grant permission for the celebration of Mass in a private cemetery chapel or in any other private oratory unless he (personally or through another ecclesiastic) has inspected the oratory and found it becomingly arranged and equipped for the offering of the august Sacrifice. As this inspection is identical with that prescribed for semi-public oratories by canon 1192, § 2,[12] which was examined in

---

10 Cappello, *De Sacramentis,* I, n. 750.

11 When granted, this privilege may be used in any decent place, certainly, therefore, in a private oratory. From this it is evident that the privilege of a portable altar is more extensive than that of a private oratory which it may be said to include, for "Plus semper in se continet quod est minus" (R. J. 35 in VI).

12 In fact, express reference is made to this canon.

the last chapter, it requires no comment here. Attention, however, is directed to the fact that when the Ordinary permits Mass in virtue of the power granted by canon 1194, he is not obliged to restrict his concession to Low Masses, as there is no indication of such a restriction of his power. Thus, for example, if all the conditions of this canon are verified, and the local Ordinary permits a newly ordained priest to offer his first holy Mass in a private oratory of his home, he can allow this Mass to be a "Missa cantata" or even a "Missa solemnis."

In view of the restrictions imposed by canon 1194, it is evident that the Ordinary's power over private oratories[13] is very limited. These restrictions, in reality, are tantamount to reserving the power of permitting Mass in a private oratory to the Holy See, as the powers for exceptional cases which it grants the Ordinary only emphasize the fact that usually he does not enjoy them. Hence, in its general results, canon 1194 can be considered as a repetition of the "Quanta cura" of the Council of Trent despite the fact that the latter expressed only a prohibition, whereas the canon formally concedes a right or power; for excluding the exceptional cases mentioned, the Code still maintains that an indult (or privilege) from the Holy See is required for the celebration of Mass in a private oratory. It is to oratories that possess such an indult that canon 1195 is devoted.

§ 1. In oratoriis domesticis ex indulto Apostolicae Sedis, nisi aliud in eodem indulto expresse caveatur, celebrari potest, postquam Ordinarius oratorium visitaverit et probaverit ad normam can. 1192, § 2, unica Missa, eaque lecta, singulis diebus, exceptis festis sollemnioribus; sed aliae functiones ecclesiasticae ibidem ne fiant.

§ 2. Ordinarius vero, dummodo iustae adsint et rationabiles causae, diversae ab eis ob quas indultum concessum fuit, etiam sollemnioribus festis permittere potest per modum actus Missae celebrationem (can. 1195).

---

13 Except over private episcopal chapels and private cemetery chapels, both of which exceptions have been sufficiently stressed.

This canon summarizes the principal regulations usually given in an Apostolic indult permitting the celebration of Mass in a private oratory. The canon, however, explicitly states that if the indult contains other provisions (conceding greater or lesser rights) the particular prescriptions of the indult and not the general regulations of this canon are to be observed.

The indult permitting the celebration of Mass in a private oratory (commonly known as an indult of a private oratory) according to the existing law [14] is conceded by the Congregation of Sacraments.[15] The petition for the indult is to be sent through the local Ordinary as it usually will not be granted unless it is accompanied by his recommendation; [16] for the indult of a private oratory is a special privilege which the Holy See will not concede unless it is convinced of the merits or need of the petitioner. The rescript conceding the indult is addressed almost invariably not to the petitioner but to the local Ordinary; [17] the reason for this practice is to be found in the fact that, according to canon 1195, § 1, the privilege of the indult cannot be used until the oratory has been inspected and approved by the Ordinary or his delegate.[18] The rescript is issued in what is known as "forma gratiosa mixta" in virtue of which the Ordinary is the executor of the rescript but is not allowed to withhold the privilege it concedes if the reasons alleged in the petition and the conditions exacted by the rescript are verified.[19] If he refuses to execute the rescript, the petitioner has

---

14 Reference will be made later to those who by privilege can concede this indult.

15 Cf. can. 249, § 2; Pius X, const. "*Sapienti concilio,*" June 29, 1908, § 1, 3°, n. 2 (Fontes, 682); "*Ordo Servandus in Curia Romana,*" Pars Altera, c. 7, art. 3, n. 10, b (Acta Apostolicae Sedis, I [1909], 86).

16 Cf. Gasparri, *De SS. Eucharistia,* I, n. 235; A Coronata, *De Locis et Temp. Sacris,* n. 88.

17 Formerly it was sent directly to the petitioner; cf. Ferraris, *Bibliotheca,* V, s. v. "Oratorium," n. 6.

18 This inspection is the same as that prescribed for semi-public oratories by can. 1192, § 2; it is demanded both by the above canon and by a clause contained in all indults.

19 Cf. can. 51 and 54; Barin, *Commentarium, Eph. Liturg.,* XL (1926), 69; A Coronata, *De Locis et Temp. Sacris,* n. 90.

the right of recourse to the Holy See, but meanwhile Mass cannot be celebrated in the oratory. If, however, he executes it, canon 1195 states that one Low Mass may be celebrated daily except on the more solemn feast days.

The Mass, therefore, must be a Low Mass ("Missa lecta"). Hence, even though the indult does not contain the word "lecta" in the usual clause "unam tantum Missam pro unoquoque die," this omission cannot be interpreted as conceding the right of celebrating a High Mass, for as Many [20] pertinently observes: "Missa cantata celebrari nequit in his oratoriis; quum enim missa sollemnis sit res valde gravis, ex eo quod indultum de ea sileat, concludi debet, praesertim sic rem interpretante consuetudine,[21] eam non concedi." But if the indult explicitly permitted the celebration of High Mass, this very exceptional privilege could be used in virtue of the saving clause of canon 1195 ("nisi aliud in eodem expresse caveatur") and the general principles of the Code on privileges contrary to law.

There are several cases in which a plurality of Masses is lawful in a private oratory: 1) If the indult expressly grants this right. 2) If Mass is offered in a private oratory by a cardinal in virtue of the privilege granted him by canon 239, § 1, 14°, his Mass does not exclude the usual daily Mass conceded by the indult. 3) In cases of grave necessity, for example, if a second Mass would be required to obtain Holy Viaticum for the dying.[22] 4) If the indult permits Mass on the Feast of Christmas, not only one but three Masses may be celebrated, even if the indult does not explicitly mention this additional privilege.[23] This was stated by the Congregation of the Council [24] concerning the indults granted to priests because of sickness;

20 *De Locis Sacris*, n. 94, 6°.

21 An even stronger argument than custom is now afforded by the clear prescription of can. 1195.

22 S. R. C., Aug. 27, 1836, § 7; D. A., 2745.

23 But none of these Masses may be celebrated on Christmas night contrary to can. 821 unless the indult grants also this right.

24 Jan. 20, 1725; this decree is quoted by Benedict XIV, *De SS. Missae Sacrificio*, L. 3, c. 4, n. 7.

by Benedict XIV [25] concerning the indults of any infirm persons; and authors extend these interpretations to any private oratory possessing the privilege of Mass on this day irrespective of the reason in virtue of which the privilege was conceded. Thus Ferreres writes: "Si quacumque ex causa concederetur Sacrum fieri in die Natalis Domini, tunc liceret illa die tres Missas ibi celebrare." [26] This liberal interpretation of authors is of little consequence for the Feast of Christmas, for, as a rule, only indults for the infirm allow Mass on this day. But when authors [27] apply it to All Souls' Day, it becomes of practical importance, as no indult prohibits Mass on this day. Of the authors consulted,[28] Blat is the only one who denies that three Masses may be offered in private oratories on All Souls' Day, and he does so only briefly and *en passant*: "Unica Missa (permittitur), etiam die Commemorationis omnium fidelium defunctorum."[29] Thus he neither enters upon a discussion of the case, nor refers to the certain exception of a plurality of Masses on Christmas which is enjoyed at least by some private oratories. Hence, until the Holy See declares otherwise, it would seem safe to follow the authors who maintain that three Masses are permissible in these oratories on All Souls' Day; certainly a priest need not hesitate to offer three Masses in a private oratory on this day if he could not otherwise trinate as he is entitled to do by canon 806, § 1.

---

25 Ep. encycl. "*Magno cum,*" June 2, 1751, § 18; Fontes, 413.

26 *Compendium Theol. Moral.*, I, n. 438. Cf. also Gasparri, *De SS. Eucharistia*, I, 235; Many, *De Locis Sacris*, n. 88; Mocchegiani, *Jurisprudentia Eccl.*, II, n. 802; A Coronata, *De Locis et Temp. Sacris*, n. 87; Cappello, *De Sacramentis*, I, n. 731; Pruemmer, *Manuale Theol. Moral.*, III, n. 284; Zitelli, *Apparatus*, L. 2, c. 3, art. 2.

27 Among the authors who make this application are Ferreres, A Coronata and Cappello (cf. references given in note 26), Barin (*Commentarium, Eph. Liturg.*, XL [1926], 69) and an anonymous consultor of the *Eph. Liturg.*, (XXXV [1921], 386).

28 Many of them do not refer to this question which was not of general interest until the const. "*Incruentum*" of Benedict XV (Aug. 10, 1915; Fontes, 706) gave all priests of the Latin Rite the faculty to trinate on All Souls' Day.

29 *Commentarium*, IV, n. 48.

The feast days on which Mass is prohibited in a private oratory are specifically enumerated in some indults, though frequently the indult contains only a general clause similar to that of canon 1195: "Exceptis festis sollemnioribus." The Congregation of Rites on April 10, 1896,[30] having been asked which days are to be considered as the more solemn feasts on which Mass is forbidden in all private oratories that have only an ordinary indult that does not specify these feasts, gave the following response: "Illi per se sunt sollemniores, in casu, qui describuntur in Caeremoniali Episcoporum, L. II, c. XXXIV, § 2, et de praecepto servantur." Hence, according to this decision, the feasts must be mentioned in the "Caeremoniale" and be feasts of precept before they exclude Mass in a private oratory.[31]

According to canon 1247, § 1, the following days (besides all Sundays) are feasts of precept: Christmas, the Circumcision of our Lord, Epiphany, the Ascension of our Lord, Corpus Christi, the Immaculate Conception of the Blessed Virgin Mary, her Assumption, the Feast of St. Joseph, the Feast of Sts. Peter and Paul and the Feast of All Saints. Easter and Pentecost are not expressly named in this canon as they always fall on a Sunday. Of these twelve feasts, only the Circumcision and Corpus Christi are not mentioned in the "Caeremoniale;" the other ten, therefore, exclude Mass in a private oratory unless the contrary is stated in the indult. Though not feasts of precept, the last three days of Holy Week must be added to this list, for without a special privilege private Masses are forbidden in all oratories on these days.[32] In the United States according to an indult obtained by the Fathers of the III Plenary Council of Baltimore,[33] the Feasts of Epiphany, Corpus Christi, St.

---

30 D. A., 3896.

31 Cf. *Eph. Liturg.*, XXXV (1921), 384; Blat, *Commentarium*, IV, n. 48; *Commentarium pro Religiosis*, III (1922), 64.

32 Cf. above, Chapter VIII, Article 4.

33 Cf. *Concilii Plenarii Baltimorensis III Acta et Decreta, n. 111;* the indult referred to was granted on Dec. 31, 1885, and is quoted in the *Acta*, p. cv.

Joseph and Sts. Peter and Paul are not feasts of precept,[34] and this indult remains in force in virtue of canon 1247, § 3. Consequently in the private oratories of our country, Mass may be celebrated on all the days of the year except Christmas, Maundy Thursday, Good Friday, Holy Saturday, Easter, Ascension, Pentecost, the Feasts of the Assumption and of the Immaculate Conception of the Blessed Virgin and All Saints' Day.

But even on these more solemn feasts, canon 1195, § 2 states that the Ordinary may permit the celebration of Mass: 1) "Dummodo iustae adsint et rationabiles causae, diversae ab eis ob quas indultum concessum fuit." The Code demands that the causes be different from those that induced the concession of the indult, as otherwise the Ordinary would be granting permission patently against the will of the Holy See which forbade the holy Sacrifice on these days despite the reasons given in the petition for the indult. 2) "Per modum actus." As this clause was examined above in connection with canon 1194, it requires no comment here. These two limitations placed upon the power of the Ordinary are identical with those stated in a decision of the Congregation of Sacraments, March 22, 1915.[35]

Indults of private oratories conceded to priests for their convenience in celebrating Mass usually specify the feasts on which Mass is prohibited therein, and very frequently these days are less numerous than those indicated above; generally the indults in favor of sick or aged priests exclude only the last three days of Holy Week. Indults conceded to the laity for their convenience in attending Mass usually exclude all the more

---

34 The external solemnity of the Feast of Sts. Peter and Paul is transferred to the following Sunday, but this cannot be shown to constitute this Sunday among the prohibited days. Cf. S. R. C., March 6, and Dec. 4, 1896 (D. A., 3890 and 3933); A Coronata, *De Locis et Temp. Sacris*, 87; Many, *De Locis Sacris*, n. 88, 3°. As the Feast of Corpus Christi does not exclude Mass in a private oratory even where it is a feast of precept, the Sunday to which its external solemnity is transferred (in the United States) certainly does not do so.

35 Cf. *Acta Apostolicae Sedis*, VII (1915), 147.

solemn feasts by a general clause, thus reminding them that at least on these days they should heed the admonition of canon 467, § 2 and attend Mass in their parish church. Another important but obvious difference exists between the oratories of the laity and those of priests. In the oratories of the laity any priest having the ordinary faculty (a *celebret*) to offer Mass in the diocese can be requested to offer the "Missa unica," but in the oratory of a priest the right of offering Mass is limited to the priest for whose convenience in celebrating the holy Sacrifice the indult was granted. In all private oratories the Mass that is celebrated must be in conformity with the calendar of the celebrant.[36]

The last subject to be considered regarding holy Mass has reference to the persons who can fulfil the obligation of a preceptive Mass by attendance in a private oratory. The Code offers only a few departures from the pre-existing discipline and these have reference to private cemetery chapels and to the private oratories of cardinals and bishops in which all who attend Mass can fulfil the precept (can. 1189 and 1249). In all other private oratories only those persons can fulfil their obligation to whom this privilege is conceded by the indult and those servants whose presence is necessary for the convenience of the privileged persons or for the service of the celebrant. As was stated above,[37] the indult usually grants this right not only to the principally privileged persons (that is, persons expressly named in the indult), but also to their relatives by consanguinity or affinity to the fourth degree inclusive, provided they live with the principally privileged persons as members of the family; it also as a rule is extended to the noble guests of the principally privileged persons.

There is one important exception to the law that all ecclesiastical functions except Mass are forbidden in private oratories despite the apparently general prohibi-

---

36 Cf. S. R. C., May 22, 1896, and Feb. 11, 1910; D. A., 3910 and 4248; Brehm, *Synopsis*, p. 213; Wapelhorst, *Compendium*, n. 36.

37 Cf. Chapter VI, Article 2, Section 1, n. 2.

tion of canon 1195, § 1: "Sed aliae functiones ecclesiasticae ibidem ne fiant." This exception is the distribution of Holy Communion as is evident from canon 869: "Sacra communio distribui potest ubicunque Missam celebrare licet, etiam in oratorio privato, nisi loci Ordinarius iustis de causis, in casibus particularibus id prohibuerit." In virtue of the unequivocal wording of this canon, the comment of Augustine to canon 1195, § 1, is misleading when he alleges the right to distribute Holy Communion in a private oratory as his private opinion: "No matter what canonists formerly held, *we believe* that, since frequent Communion is so strongly urged, the distribution of the Eucharist would not be forbidden (in private oratories). At any rate, *the permission of the bishop would suffice.*"[38] That Holy Communion may be distributed in private oratories is no longer a mere opinion, it is a certain right that has been recognized by law since the general decree of the Congregation of Rites in 1907.[39] As also the Code clearly concedes and proclaims this right, the permission of the bishop (local Ordinary) is superfluous; he indeed may forbid the exercise of this right, but only in particular cases (hence, not by a general statute) and for a just cause, as he may do regarding even public oratories and churches.

Other exceptions to the general prohibition of canon 1195, § 1 are made by the Code in its tract on the sacraments; these, however, are of minor consequence, as they either do not occur frequently, or when they do occur, the sacraments in question can be administered not only in a private oratory but also in any other becoming place. These exceptions are the following:[40] 1) Baptism may be administered privately anywhere in case of necessity (can. 771); certainly, therefore, in a private oratory; It may be administered solemnly in a private oratory if the rulers of the country or their prospective successors re-

---

38 *Commentary,* VI, 83. The italics in the citation are not his.

39 May, 8; D. A., 4201.

40 They were made also in the pre-Code law; cf. above, Chapter VI, Article 2, Section 1, n. 4-5.

quest this privilege (from the local Ordinary or pastor) in behalf of their children or grandchildren, or if the local Ordinary grants it to other persons in an extraordinary case (can. 776). 2) Though the proper place for administering the sacrament of Penance is the confessional in a church, public or semi-public oratory, still the confessions of men may be heard in a private oratory; confessions of women may be heard there only in case of necessity (can. 908-910). 3) Matrimony may be celebrated in a private oratory with the permission of the local Ordinary which should be granted only in an extraordinary case and for a just and reasonable cause (can. 1109, § 2); under these conditions he may grant also the right of the nuptial Mass.[41] Finally, functions that are altogether extra-liturgical (e. g., the recitation of prayers, novenas, etc.) even though they are conducted by a priest are not forbidden,[42] for such functions—or rather devotions—are licit everywhere, certainly, therefore, in a private oratory. It is evident that of the few exceptions that can be urged to the general prohibition of canon 1195, the distribution of Holy Communion is by far the most important.

It may not be amiss here to call attention to canon 1282, § 1 which forbids the keeping of important relics [43] of the Saints or Blessed in private homes or private oratories without the express permission of the local Ordinary. The Church wishes these relics as a rule to be accessible to the veneration of all the faithful, a desire that cannot be realized if they are preserved in a private oratory.

As was stated above, the indult of a private oratory according to the existing law is conceded by the Congregation of Sacraments. The Holy See, however, gives some local Ordinaries the special faculty of granting a

41 S. R. C., Aug. 31, 1872, § 3; D. A., 3265.

42 Cf. Barin, *Commentarium*, *Eph. Liturg.*, XL (1926), 71.

43 "Insignes Sanctorum vel Beatorum reliquiae sunt corpus, caput, brachium, antibrachium, cor, lingua, manus, crus aut illa pars corporis in qua passus est martyr, dummodo sit integra et non parva" (can. 1281, § 2).

similar indult within the territory over which they exercise jurisdiction. This faculty (contained in the more extensive faculty of conceding the right of a portable altar) has been procured by the Congregation of the Propaganda for the local Ordinaries in mission territory.[44] It rarely is conceded to the Ordinaries of fully organized dioceses and is not contained in the quinquennial faculties of our bishops. Our Apostolic Delegate, however, has the faculty "Concedendi sacerdotibus infirmis, durante infirma valetudine, aut aetate devexis indultum oratorii privati, in quo Missam celebrent, servatis canonicis regulis."[45] As no exemplar of an indult of a private oratory has been given thus far, it may be of interest to cite the following which is a literal copy of an original concession from our Apostolic Delegate:

> Illustrissime ac Reverendissime Domine:
>
> Rev. mus D. mus N. N., Sacerdos dioecesis N., infirmae valetudinis causa, expostulet privilegium Oratorii Privati.
>
> Et Deus etc.
>
> ---
>
> Vigore specialium facultatum Nobis ab Apostolica Sede concessarum, Oratori benigne indulgemus ut in domo suae privatae habitationis, in loco tamen a domesticis et profanis usibus segregato, erigere possit Oratorium Privatum, decenter instructum et ornatum, ac prius ab Ordinario loci vel ab alio sacerdote de eius licentia visitandum et approbandum, in quo Missam singulis diebus etiam sollemnioribus celebrare valeat; exceptis Nocte Nativitatis Dominicae et tribus ultimis feriis hebdomadae majoris; quae quidem Missa etiam inservienti et familiaribus in ecclesiastici praecepti adimplementum suffragetur. Salvis semper juribus parochialibus. Praesentibus tantum tempore infirmitatis et non ultra quinquennium valituris.
>
> Datum Washingtonii, ex Aedibus Delegationis Apostolicae, die——.
>
> (Sigillum)
>
> Delegatus Apostolicus.

---

[44] Cf. the faculties quoted by Vermeersch-Creusen, *Epitome,* I, n. 814, Appendix II, A, n. 4.

[45] Cf. the faculties quoted by Vermeersch-Creusen, *Epitome,* I, n. 813, Appendix I, c. IV, n. 34.

The following points are noteworthy in this indult: 1) Even though the grantee moves to a different diocese, he still enjoys the privilege conceded in the indult, as it omits the usual clause restricting the grant to the diocese in which he resides at the time of its concession. But whenever he moves to a new dwelling, whether temporarily or permanently, whether in or outside of his present diocese, the visitation and approval of the local Ordinary or his delegate as prescribed by canon 1195, § 1, is necessary before he may offer Mass the first time in the new oratory.[46] 2) This indult exemplifies the assertion made above that infirm priests usually are granted the privilege of offering Mass on all days of the year except the last three days of Holy Week. The phrase "Nocte Nativitatis Dominicae" excludes Mass only on Christmas night, not on Christmas day. 3) The indult is granted for a maximum period of five years during which time its use is conditioned on the infirmity of the grantee.

There are a number of persons who enjoy the right of a private oratory in virtue of their dignity or office. Cardinals and bishops (residential and titular) frequently have been mentioned in these pages as enjoying this right in virtue of canons 239, § 1, 7°, 18°, 349, § 1 and 1189, the last mentioned canon giving their private oratories all the additional rights and privileges of semi-public oratories. The *Motu proprio* of Pius X, *"Inter multiplices,"*[47] states that the indult of a private oratory is enjoyed by the Prothonotaries Apostolic *de numero participantium,* the Prothonotaries *supranumerarii* and the Prothonotaries *ad instar,* and according to canon 4 this concession is still valid. The oratories of these dignitaries, however, do not enjoy the rights and privileges of semi-public oratories as do those of cardinals and bishops, though all who attend Mass in the oratories of

46 This new approval must be obtained even if the oratory is transferred only from one room to another in the same house. Cf. Many, *De Locis Sacris,* n. 97.

47 Feb. 21, 1905, § § 11, 22 and 46; *Acta Sanctae Sedis,* XXXVII (1905), 491; Fontes, 665.

the Prothonotaries *de numero participantium* fulfil the obligation of a preceptive Mass, as this additional right is clearly stated in the concession to these prelates,[48] and is recognized by canon 1249. The private oratories of Vicars and Prefects Apostolic and of Apostolic Administrators also possess this special right in virtue of canons 308 and 315.

§ 1. Oratoria domestica nec consecrari nec benedici possunt more ecclesiarum.

§ 2. Licet oratoria domestica et semi-publica communi locorum domorumve benedictione aut nulla benedictione donentur, debent tamen esse divino tantum cultui reservata et ab omnibus domesticis usibus libera (can. 1196).

The prohibition of this canon to consecrate or solemnly bless private oratories is identical with that of the general decree of the Congregation of Rites of June 5, 1899: "Sacra Rituum Congregatio mandat, ut nullum ex oratoriis privatis consecretur, aut Benedictione donetur sollemni, quae in Rituali Romano legitur; sed ea tantum formula benedicatur, quae pro domo nova aut loco in eodem Rituali habetur."[49] Both this decree and the Code refer to the ordinary "Benedictio Loci vel Domus"[50] as the formula to be used if a private oratory is to be blessed; but owing to the fact that the Roman Ritual as revised since the promulgation of the Code contains a special blessing for private oratories, the "Benedictio Oratorii Privati seu Domestici,"[51] it would seem more becoming to use this blessing in preference to any other. These blessings are only invocative, not constitutive, and none is prescribed; hence private oratories are not sacred places as defined by canon 1154, and consequently do not enjoy the rights of sacred places.

---

48 As is also their exemption from the jurisdiction of the local Ordinary; hence their oratories are not subject to his inspection and approval.

49 § 6; D. A., 4025.

50 *Rituale Romanum*, Tit. 8, c. 6.

51 Appendix, *Benedictiones non reservatae*, n. 16. Formerly this blessing was reserved to the diocese of Lyons; cf. Barin, *Commentarium*, *Eph. Liturg.*, XL (1926), 72.

Finally, canon 1196, § 2 prescribes that a private oratory be reserved exclusively for divine worship even if it has received no blessing whatsoever. This law requires no further comment as it was examined in the last chapter and its topic was referred to repeatedly in these pages. It is indeed most appropriate that the last law of the Code in its tract on oratories should be devoted to this subject, thereby giving another example of the constant zeal of the Church for the holiness of the House of God; for even an unblessed oratory by the celebration of the holy Sacrifice of the Mass truly becomes a "Domus Dei," concerning which the Psalmist wrote three thousand years ago: "Domum tuam decet sanctitudo, Domine, in longitudinem dierum."[52]

---

52 Ps. XCII, 5.

DEUS LUX MEA

THESES

QUAS

AD DOCTORATUS GRADUM

IN

IURE CANONICO

Apud Universitatem Catholicam Americae

CONSEQUENDUM

PUBLICE PROPUGNABIT

ALOISIUS HERMANUS FELDHAUS

SACERDOS CONGREGATIONIS PRETIOSISSIMI SANGUINIS

IURIS CANONICI LICENTIATUS

HORA XI A. M. DIE XXV MAII A. D. MCMXXVII

EX IURE PUBLICO ECCLESIASTICO.

I. De Forma Regiminis in Ecclesia.

II. De Relatione inter Ecclesiam et Statum.

III. De Concordatis.

EX IURE CANONICO.

IV. De Historia Iuris Canonici.

V. Canones 1-7 Normae Introductoriae.

VI. Canones 8-24 De Legibus Ecclesiasticis.

VII. Canones 25-30 De Consuetudine.

VIII. Canones 31-35 De Temporis Supputatione.

IX. Canones 36-62 De Rescriptis.

X. Canones 63-79 De Privilegiis.

XI. Canones 80-86 De Dispensationibus.

XII. Canones 87-90, 107 De Personarum Natura et Divisione.

XIII. Canones 92-95 De Domicilio et Quasi-Domicilio.

XIV. Canones 329-333 De Nominatione et Institutione Episcoporum.

XV. Canones 451-470 De Officio Parochorum.

XVI. Canones 492-498 De Erectione et Suppressione Religionis, Provinciae, Domus.

XVII. Canones 499-517 De Superioribus et de Capitulis.

XVIII. Canones 518-530 De Confessariis et Cappellanis.

XIX. Canones 539-541 De Postulatu.

XX. Canones 542-552 De Requisitis ut quis in Novitiatum Admittatur.

XXI. Canones 553-571 De Novitiorum Institutione.

XXII. Canones 572-586 De Professione Religiosa.

XXIII. Canones 770-776 De Tempore et Loco Baptismi Conferendi.

XXIV. Canones 820-823 De Tempore et Loco Missae Celebrandae.

XXV. Canones 1012-1018 De Natura Matrimonii et de Sponsalitiis.

XXVI. Canones 1058-1080 De Impedimentis Matrimonialibus.

XXVII. Canones 1081-1093 De Consensu Matrimoniali.

XXVIII. Canones 1118-1127 De Dissolutione Vinculi.

XXIX. Canones 1161-1187 De Ecclesiis.

XXX. Canones 1188-1196 De Oratoriis.

XXXI. Canones 1265-1275 De Custodia et Cultu SS. Eucharistiae.

XXXII. Canones 1960-1992 De Causis Matrimonialibus.

XXXIII. Canones 2147-2161 De Remotione Parochorum.

XXXIV. Canones 2162-2167 De Translatione Parochorum.

XXXV. Canones 2168-2175 De Modo Procedendi contra Clericos non residentes.

XXXVI. Canones 2186-2194 De Modo Procedendi in Suspensione ex Informata Conscientia Infligenda.

XXXVII. Canones 2195-2198 De Natura Delicti eiusque Divisione.

XXXVIII. Canones 2215-2219 De Poenarum Notione, Speciebus, Interpretatione atque Applicatione.

XXXIX. Canones 2220-2225 De Superiore Potestatem Coactivam Habente.

XL. Canones 2236-2240 De Remissione Poenarum.

ROMAN LAW.

XLI. Periods of Roman Law.
XLII. The *Corpus Juris Civilis;* Sources and Division.
XLIII. Elements of Personality.
XLIV. Citizenship.
XLV. Liberty and Slavery.
XLVI. Manumission.
XLVII. *Res Mancipi* and *Nec Mancipi.*
XLVIII. Marriage.
XLIX. The Roman Family.
L. Division and Acquisition of Things.
LI. Juridical Position of Women.
LII. Adoption and Adrogation.

INTERNATIONAL LAW.

LIII. Nature and Sources of International Law.
LIV. Rights and Obligations of Sovereign States.
LV. Methods of Acquiring Territorial Jurisdiction.
LVI. Treaties; Nature and Kinds.
LVII. Diplomatic Agents; Immunities and Privileges.
LVIII. Amicable Settlement of International Disputes; non-hostile Redress.
LIX. Status of Persons in War; Combatants and Non-combatants.
LX. The Monroe Doctrine.

VIDIT FACULTAS:

PHILIPPUS BERNARDINI, S.T.D., J.U.D., Decanus.
LUDOVICUS MOTRY, S.T.D., J.C.D., a Secretis.
VALENTINUS SCHAAF, O.F.M., J.C.D.
FRANCISCUS LARDONE, S.T.D., J.U.D.
MANOEL DE OLIVIERA LIMA, L.H.B.

VIDIT RECTOR UNIVERSITATIS:

✠THOMAS J. SHAHAN, S.T.D., J.U.L., LL.D.

VITA.

Aloysius Herman Feldhaus was born in Louisville, Kentucky, August 11, 1896. After attending the parochial school of St. Martin, he entered St. Joseph's College, Collegeville, Indiana, where he pursued the academic and collegiate courses under the direction of the Fathers of the Society of the Most Precious Blood. In September of 1917 he entered St. Charles Seminary, Carthagena, Ohio, and was received into the Society of the Most Precious Blood. On May 13, 1923, he was ordained to the Holy Priesthood, and for the next two years was engaged in teaching in the collegiate department of St. Charles Seminary. In September of 1925 he registered in the School of Canon Law of the Catholic University of America. He takes this opportunity to express his gratitude to the professors who have assisted him with their kind suggestions.

www.ingramcontent.com/pod-product-compliance
Lightning Source LLC
LaVergne TN
LVHW050214080826
844660LV00012B/409

* 9 7 8 0 8 1 3 2 2 2 3 1 8 *